"Doug Giles is a good man, and his bambinas are fearless. His girls Hannah and Regis Giles are indefatigable. I admire the Giles clan from afar."

– Dennis Miller

"Doug Giles must be some kind of a great guy if CNN wants to impugn him."

– Rush Limbaugh

"Doug Giles is a substantive and funny force for traditional values."

– Ann Coulter, best-selling author

Don't read this book! That is, don't read this book if you are content living indecisively. Don't read this book if you are pleased with the current, cultural state of affairs. In short, don't read this book if you are satisfied with your life. However, if you are fed up with mediocrity and are looking for much-needed inspiration and information on how and why your life can make a difference for Christ and his ever-expanding kingdom, then "take up read."

Dennis Darville,
Lead Pastor - Christ Covenant Church

"Doug Giles speaks the truth ... he's a societal watchdog ... a funny bastard."

– Ted Nugent, rock icon

If you think we are living in the "End Times" and that God is going to "rapture" you out of this mess at any minute, then this book is for you. It'll challenge that notion. If you think Christianity is only for the weak minded, then this book is for you. Buckle up. If you're tired of watching our nation sink into the abyss of immorality, socialism, and atheism and you want to do something about it, then this book is for you! It's a blueprint to turn this nation around. Like the reformers who transformed nations in the past, Doug Giles challenges Christians to follow these 10 specific biblical disciplines that have been proven to change nations and ultimately the world. Doug's message is not for the faint of heart, however, so you might be offended at times. Which is good and very necessary when God's people have become immoral, lazy, fat and stupid. King Solomon wisely said, "Faithful are the wounds of a friend; but the kisses of an enemy are deceitful." Read and apply Doug's Rules for Radical Christians to your life and watch God change you from just another butt in a pew, to a powerful believer that terrifies the powers of darkness.

Brandon Vallorani
Founder & CEO, Romulus
Marketing & Vallorani Estates,
Author of, The Wolves and the Mandolin (Forbes Books)

Doug is on fire in this no-holds-barred book that will surely upset the nominal Christians of our times! I will be using it to help train the youth and young adults in our church to engage and impact our society. It's biblical, practical, and powerful!

Rich Witmer
Lead Pastor - Destiny Church.
Co-host of Warriors and Wildmen.

In RULES FOR RADICAL CHRISTIANS, Doug Giles demonstrates his knowledge and love for the Word of God and his concern for the youth of our country. Doug utilizes his humor and life experiences to penetrate the mind and soul of a reader that would otherwise not be reached. This book should be read and absorbed by every member of the family.

Tron Simpson
Host of 'The Tron Show'

Published by White Feather Press.
(www.whitefeatherpress.com)

ISBN 978-1-61808-172-8

Printed in the United States of America

Cover design by David Bugnon and mobopolis.com

Editing by Steve 'Stevie Joe' Pauwels

Rules for Radical Christians

*10 Biblical Disciplines
for Influential Believers*

Written by
Doug Giles

Table of Contents

Foreword

Indeed, there are huge, heavy-caliber issues over which Christians have been locking horns for a long time – for centuries in fact: exactly how much are people who love Jesus supposed to impact, for His glory, every part of life around them? Beyond that, how can the faithful carry out that "impacting" without being overcome by the world system or corrupted by its ways? In *Rules for Radical Christians: 10 Biblical Disciplines for Influential Believers* author Doug Giles, in his own puckish and inimitable way, gives a big thumbs up to: a) why God's people are supposed to effectively penetrate and influence every part of human existence; and b) how, in the process, every believer must take practical steps to protect himself or herself from the pernicious seductions of secularism, humanism, atheism or cowardly concessions of any kind.

Hide-in-the-pews churchgoers won't find Doug's counsel to be a comforting read. Sterile but safe religiosity? Definitely in his cross-hairs. Conversely, those who take the call to be "salt and light" to a desperately needy world as an excuse to act like that same world will be challenged to wake up and grow up. Be tough but don't sell out righteousness; keep the Kingdom of God priority number one, always; seek God's approval above all, not the accolades of flawed fellow human beings.

If every follower of Christ on the planet were to read *Rules for Radical Christians*, take its prescriptions to heart and put them to use starting today? Watch out, history! A spiritual revolution would commence a-brewing ... stat. Exactly what Jesus intended, in fact.

So, snoozing saints, compromising Christians, bone-headed believers beware: *Rules for Radical Christians* might just ring your bell.

Wherever necessary, may the God who created men to change the world for His plans and purposes make it so.

Steve Pauwels
Senior Pastor, Church of The King

Dedication

This book is dedicated to Christians who refuse to sit on the sidelines of life and pick lint out of their Christian navel, but instead, want to infiltrate culture and turn the kingdoms of this world into, The Kingdom of our God and Christ. For those about to rock, I salute you. #boom

Preface

Much of the material in *Rules for Radical Christians* has been taken from scripts written for an audiobook I performed and produced many moons ago.

The spoken form has been retained, so expect the rules of grammar to be more violated than the lines in Hillary Clinton's 2016 Christmas coloring book.

In regards to the brief and flimsy way I handle the weighty topics platformed within … please … cut me some slack. My intent is to, perhaps, be a "first word," or an "in addition to," rather than the "last."

If I can get you to think, then I'm happy.

Doug Giles,
April Fool's Day, 2018
Somewhere in Texas

"There is no problem with the wider culture that you cannot see in spades in the Christian Church. The rot is in us, and not simply out there. And Christians are making a great mistake by turning everything into culture wars. It's a much deeper crisis."

— Os Guinness

Introduction

Our Utmost for His Highest
I love it when lazy and chunky, willfully ignorant and politically inactive, self-obsessed and culturally ineffective "Christians" complain about "how bad things are getting," and how this must be "the end of the world" principally because Kim Kardashian is making mad money off her Instagram butt pics.

Yep, these myopic seers of only bad omens think humanity has never seen the likes of our kind of vice, and, thus, they conclude, "The End has come."

When I hear these goobers talk about the supposed "never-before-seen depravity" and their conclusion that this must be what R.E.M. sang about in their 1987 smash hit, *It's The End Of The World*, I'm like, "Have you ever studied world history even a wee bit? Have you ever picked up your Bible and just read the chapter titles? Huh?"

Look, not-so-sharp Christian, it's been bad before. Like in real bad. And you know what? The world didn't end. It kept clipping along.

God's solution for cultural pollution has always been His people's shaping up their shoddy spiritual lives and becoming purposefully engaged in re-forming the sinful deformities besetting this blue marble. Shocking, eh?

By the way, a lot of the biblical and post-biblical reformers had a much worse field to plow than we do. As we'll see in this little book, our protagonists didn't have the incredible props that we have, and their milieu was way more antagonistic toward their faith.

For instance, Twenty-six-hundred years ago, the nation of Judah was finding it inconvenient to follow the Law of God. After Jehovah patiently warned this backslidden bunch through His prophets, He finally got sick of their contumacy. He decided that if they wouldn't listen to His prophets – maybe they would listen to seventy years of getting their backsides handed to them by a godless king named, Nebuchadnezzar.

Nebuchadnezzar was one of the top guns of the ancient world. Imagine all the worst world leaders that are around now blended into one megalomaniacal fiend on steroids. That's Nebuchadnezzar. God chose this wicked king and kingdom to smack Judah back to obedience to His holy covenant. Nebuchadnezzar ransacked the people of God. He wrecked their Precious Moments figurine collections. Every sweet, little religious ditty that they held dear met the Babylonian wood-chipper. Not only did he waylay their quaint way of life, but he dragged their butts kicking and screaming into his demonic den ... Babylon.

Babylon, though wicked, was not gnarly to a

young persons' fleshly, lower-cortex, monkey-brain delights. Imagine, if you will, a beautiful place with sort of a 24/7/365 Spring Break in Miami feel. Yep, Babylon was decadent and attractive, and if you weren't properly grounded in God you'd probably be found twerking away on a Red Bull stage doing Jello shots off a girl's chest at Nikki Beach Club.

And that, my friends, was the mise en scène Daniel, Hananiah, Mishael and Azariah were forced into.

Check it out: these teenagers (teenagers, mind you) got cut off from their Bible studies and their backyard barbecues and were tossed into a culture that wooed them daily to blow off God. To the natural eye, and from a churchy perspective, these young men were in deep yogurt. It appeared that their relationships with God, and their rightful places in the planet, were fleeing reality faster than a chalupa dipped in Lubriderm would go through your digestive tract.

Shockingly, these choice young men thrived in this scat-laden culture. It wasn't easy, though – but so what? God never said it would be easy. These young dudes, with the odds tremendously stacked against them, came through this God-ordained hailstorm with their faith intact and the wicked culture courting their righteous help and advice. Can you say, 'Boom!'"? I knew you could.

The grand ascent of Daniel and his compadres, in a sinfully complicated mess, was the product of giving God their utmost for His highest. Along with their unfeigned faith, they also pursued excellence in dealing with their bedeviled flesh. Consequently, they became leaders who were sharp, solid and smart; well-versed in all manner of knowledge and understanding in Babylon's literature and language. They were brilliant servants who were ten times greater than all in Nebuchadnezzar's kingdom.

Guess what, young Christian? It's déjà vu all over again. You are where Daniel and his buddies were 2,600 years ago – in the Babylonian environment under the sway of demonic principalities that have your erasure in mind.

That's where my book, *Rules for Radical Christians*, comes in handy. The 'tolerant' society in which you live is intolerant of your biblical worldview. So what are young people to do? You could huddle together in a Christian subculture and pray that Christ would come quickly and rapture you out of this mess. Or, you could compromise your godly principles, becoming spiritual chameleons and allow your relationship with Christ to be governed by CNN. Or, you can become strategically equipped to move into an anti-theistic environment and effectively influence it for the glory of God. *Rules for Radical Christians* argues for the last option.

Rules for Radical Christians is not a survival devotional designed to help the young adult limp through life. Rather, it is a road-tested, dominion blueprint that will equip the young adult with leadership skills and sufficient motivation to rise to a place of power in an overtly non-Christian culture just like Daniel did.

Daniel and his friends were stripped of everything that was sacred to them, renamed after devils, seduced daily and indoctrinated in an anti-theistic school system that makes our public schools look like Knox Seminary. And, yet, fair Christian, they didn't backslide, whine or join a transgendered Chaldean improv group. Instead, they became shining examples to youth for all time: proof that greatness and godly influence never depend upon living in squeaky-clean, perfect conditions. Their culture sucked and yet they turned it around. What's your excuse?

Rules for Radical Christians has come from a scriptural quest for an answer to: How can we change an aggressive, anti-theistic environment that wants jack-squat to do with Jesus Christ? Through my blog (228 million page views at this writing), my Warriors and Wildmen podcast (425k downloads in the first nine months) and speaking engagements, I have learned that young Christians want to put a dent in el Diablo's haggard backside – but they are befuddled as to where to begin.

Rules for Radical Christians focuses on clear, biblical texts to answer that confusion. I hope that after you've read this hot little tome, Satan thoroughly regrets ever messing with you as you systematically wipe out his influence in this world and turn back the kingdoms of this world to the kingdom of our Lord and of His Christ.

PART ONE

Welcome to the Jungle

"Since it is so likely that children will meet cruel enemies, let them at least have heard of brave knights and heroic courage."

– C.S. Lewis

Chapter 1
The Blunt End of the Pool Cue

"And an adulteress hunts for the precious life…"

Proverbs 6:26b

Christ must have something great in store for today's youth.

I know … I know … today's youth seem more lost than Jeff Sessions at a Kera and The Lesbians concert. Yet, at the same time (in Scripture) whenever a generation of young people got slapped around, it was actually because within that demographic lay a deliverer, like Jesus or Moses or someone else who posed a threat to Satan.

I believe the youth of today will raise up individuals who will provide the vision to lead our society to a new height of principled belief in God, to a re-freshed, ethical commitment such as has not been seen in generations.

That's why the powers of darkness are after to-day's youth. That's why Lucifer has all of his hench-men mainlining espresso and working overtime at-tempting to blind, bind and bastardize this generation of young adults.

They feel threatened by the potential of the young people on the scene even though they are immature believers. Therefore, it's sadly logical that those who do have destiny upon them to overthrow Satan's possessions will get the blunt end of the pool cue, even before they are a real threat.

With Satan's obvious, full-frontal assault being levied at this generation of young adults, we've got to make sure we don't add to his ridiculous success by unwittingly playing into his hands.

Young person, we've got to stop opting for the path of least resistance, i.e., acting like a bunch of cattle when Lucifer tempts you to take it. When he entices us to compromise the absolutes of Scripture, we must refuse to become politically correct, living a "Christianity" based upon public opinion. Also, we've got to peel our faces off the plate and cease to snort the pleasure dope when the Serpent lures us with temporary gratification over self-sacrifice and discipline.

As much as Satan is trying to sideline today's youth, we must make sure we are not assisting him, but rather thoroughly resisting him so that our names don't register on the culpability flow chart of our culture's current demise.

"Many years ago I learned an important truth: When hard times come, be a student … not a victim."

– Rick Godwin

Chapter 2. Reality Bites and So Should You!

"In the world you have tribulation, but take courage; I have overcome the world."

John 16:33

Reforming a deformed culture isn't going to be easy – but so what?

We must realize we're going to have to go against the flow and, sometimes, that can become more tiresome and nerve-wracking than listening to your sister's first violin recital. Changing society for God's glory has always been difficult … and I hate to ruin your day – but life isn't a movie.

Sometimes it bites. But isn't that the cool part? The thrill of hard work … the opposition … surmounting the odds … the possibility of an incredible victory?

According to the book of Daniel, 2,600 years ago there were four Hebrew lads who found themselves in a scatological mess. These young men didn't ignore the situation, and they didn't just pray about the Rosie-sized problems they were facing. Instead, they penetrated the highest echelon of a radical, anti-God environment, and effectively changed it for God's glory.

The youths were Daniel, Shadrach, Meshach, and Abednego, and because they rocked – we salute them. These top guns will be our protagonists as we seek God's wisdom in facing similar situations in a society that is glutted with anti-biblical sentiments.

Let me ask you something, young Christian: Don't you want to do something with your life? Don't you want your life to count?

Should liberties that were hard won over centuries of political heroism based in philosophic genius and consecrated by the blood of the martyrs find you having only two great goals in life: 1. to own a Prius and 2. to marry a girl like Anna Kendrick?

If you want to do something with your life, then this book is for you. This is for the wannabe young adult who desires to rise above the flotsam and to soar with the biblical eagles instead of flocking with the turkeys.

"Depend upon it, sir, when a man knows he is to be hanged in a fortnight, it concentrates his mind wonderfully."

– Samuel Johnson

Chapter 3. When Society Sucks Worse than an Airplane Toilet?

"For men will be lovers of self, lovers of money, boastful, arrogant, revilers, disobedient to parents, ungrateful, unholy, unloving, irreconcilable, malicious gossips, without self-control, brutal, haters of good, treacherous, reckless, conceited, lovers of pleasure rather than lovers of God…"

2 Timothy 3:2-4 NASB

The days we are living in, Daniel's Babylon, are darker than a goth chick's closet.

Though the ancient city of Babylon is gone, the spirit of Babylon – like your freaky kinfolk – just … won't … leave.

Babylon is a culture, an attitude, a system and a way of life that is diametrically opposed to the things of God. Everything the kingdom of God is, Babylon isn't.

And what's wild is, the Babylon of Daniel's day afforded him no Christian social media support groups.

Daniel had nada ... nothing ... zero ... zilch ... zippo.

He had no one and nothing to support him. As a matter of fact, the bad environment that Daniel was placed in was specially ordered by God, for His people, who were finding it inconvenient to listen to His commandments.

Nevertheless, even though dwelling in a time of chastisement, Daniel worked his way into a place of prominence by being faithful to the Lord.

You know, the fact that we are in cultural dire straits as a nation shouldn't send you screaming like a chick, or boy for that matter, to the tribulation shelter to eat canned meats and just wait on the rapture.

Just because the odds are currently stacked against us doesn't mean the end has come. Jesus might not show up as soon as everyone thinks He will.

What we can be certain of is this: no matter what our condition is, good or bad, His command to disciple the nations still stands. Therefore, we have got to ask ourselves, "Self, what does God want me to do when society sucks worse than an airplane toilet?"

Our only recourse as Christians is to go to the scripture and see what God required his people to do when times were bad and imitate. During Daniel's day, God put the prepared believer into the cacophonic, Babylonian mix to bring divine harmony to a weird kingdom gone mad.

And, young adult, this is what He wants to do with you, as well.

PART TWO

Absorb, Separate, or Infiltrate?

Chapter 4. Absorption: Christian Chameleons

"To follow Jesus is to pay the cost of discipleship, and then to die to ourselves, to our own interests, our own agendas and reputations. It is to pick up our crosses and count the cost of losing all that contradicts his will and his way—including our reputations before the world, and our standing with the people and in the communities that we once held dear. It is to live before one audience, the audience of One, and therefore to die to all other conflicting opinions and assessments. There is no room here for such contemporary ideas as the looking-glass self, and no consideration here for trivial contemporary obsessions such as one's legacy."

— Os Guinness

Whenever a believer is faced with a Babylonian environment, as was the prophet Daniel, he has three options: absorb the culture, separate from it or infiltrate it.

Let's look at the temptation to absorb the culture. Here are five signs, according to Chuck Finney, that you have been changed by your daft culture.

1. You have a never-ending search for worldly amusements. People who are always chasing pleasures, who must fill their lives with innumerable toys and must always be playing, have been consumed – eaten up – by the world. Sure, we've got to rest and play ... no argument here. What I'm thinking about is the pleasure-monger who's addicted to fun and allergic to godly duty.

2. You have a lack of enjoyment and interest in God's word. One sure sign that you're slowly absorbing too much of the world is that you are not enjoying God's presence, and your Bible is collecting dust. When the heart loves God, real communion with Him is a must. It's not a hassle.

3. You exhibit outward formality in Christian exercises. A formal way of saying and doing things, which is clearly a result of habit rather than the outflow of one's heart, is a sign of absorption. When this person sings, speaks or does anything in God's name, he does it with all the excitement of Donald Trump going to a banquet in honor of Nancy Pelosi.

4. You neglect church for slight reasons. I know that some churches are about as in-

spiring as Mitch McConnell reading Leviticus backwards in Latin after he has drunk six bottles of Nyquil. But you and I both know that there are a great number of Christ-centered, Bible-believing churches that are excited about God's word.

If just one of these gatherings takes place in a home or in a building in your city, and you know about it – and you miss it for some lame reason – then you can unrest assured that you are far away from God.

5. You have lost interest in truly spiritual conversation and/or your spiritual conversation is greatly lacking in content. When it's easier and more engaging to prattle on about any -- and everything on earth but God and His cause, there's something wrong. When our conversation comes to a screeching halt when the things of God are mentioned, or our depth of contribution in such conversation makes Mariah Carey sound like C.S. Lewis, we've got to ask ourselves, "What the heck has happened to me?" As a young Christian wanting to grind Satan's face in the gravel, absorption of the culture is totally taboo.

There are only two kinds of people: those who say to God, "Thy will be done," and those to whom God says, "All right, then, have it your way."

– C.S. Lewis

Chapter 5. Separation:
Life in the Ghetto

The second option the believer faces in a Babylonian environment is the classic overcorrection of temptation to absorb: namely, to separate from the world … retreat from society … get as far away from it as possible … create and live in a Christian ghetto.

Unlike absorption, the separation state of mind causes Christians to refuse contact with anyone outside the Church. Sinners, the media, art, music, politics, educational systems, business … all of these must be avoided in order to focus only on that which outwardly appears to benefit the Church and prepares us for the afterlife to come.

For such a retreatist to maintain this erroneous

thinking, he's got to find several Scriptures to mis-interpret in order to substantiate his distorted be-liefs. So he centers his attention only on those texts that speak of separation from the world and those that promote hanging out with just the brothers.

The separatist desires a "heart" religion. He or she wants to be pure and unsullied by the world – and understandably so. In reaction to dead religion, smarmy intellectualism and carnality in "Christians", experiencing heavenly feelings during personal Bible study while tucked away from the mean-old-world seems like the thing to do.

But there is a danger here, as well. What can happen during the process of constantly looking in-ward for correct feelings is one can get chained to the never-ending treadmill of spiritual navel-gazing and forget the command that we are to become seriously engaged in our society.

Those who separate from society focus on the shallow waters of religious slush. They have a false view of spirituality (thank you, Plato), which divides reality into two categories: that which is spiritual and that which is The Kardashians. Emphasizing irra-tionality and spirituality at the expense of rationality and reality gives the separatist a fractured view of truth … one with which the visible world is at war.

Yeah, sure, bad religion and worldliness might have removed truth from life; but an unbiblical separation from the culture by Christians has removed reality from the truth.

Those who have opted out of engaging our culture might have done so with good motives – wanting to experience more of God's presence to stay pure. Yet while becoming seemingly privately engaged with their "personal Savior", they have become socially irrelevant.

"If I sit next to a madman as he drives a car into a group of innocent bystanders, I can't, as a Christian, simply wait for the catastrophe, then comfort the wounded and bury the dead. I must try to wrestle the steering wheel out of the hands of the driver."

– Dietrich Bonhoeffer

Chapter 6. Separation: Achtung, Baby

The believer must be seriously involved with society. Separation from the world simply allows wickedness to increase. Duh.

The separatism of Germany's Church from political affairs in the 1930s allowed Hitler to wreak havoc in Europe. The "believers", focusing on their own walks with God and separating themselves from the world, did so to the destruction of everything they held dear – not to mention the lives of millions of people.

The German church (like all Christian churches) should have godly influence on the politics of the day – as God commanded. Instead, their inactivity caused there to be no effective internal resistance to Hitler.

Twentieth-century German theologian Dietrich Bonhoeffer was relentless towards the separatist mentality of the German Church in the thirties. He saw those who opted for a segregated, separate life as doing so because they had been squeezed out of the centers of political and cultural power.

He derided the thought that a Christian is to live in a little spiritual niche on the sidelines of life. Bonhoeffer said the separatists' church was an "escapist's church", a community of "salvation-egoists" that was no longer the salt of the earth or the light of the world.

As in Nazi Germany, the consequences of our lack of involvement with society can be grave.

In his excellent book, *Lambs that Roar*, Bob Briner provides a good acid test to determine whether we are socially active believers, involved with our community, or Separatists, who allow Satan free and unhindered access to God's planet – the very earth which we are commanded to steward.

Grab a pencil and paper and run through this little checklist:

1. I've attended a school board meeting or city council meeting within the last year.

2. I own at least one piece of original art.

3. I have as many close friends outside of the church as I do inside.

4. In the last year, I have written one letter of praise to a network or a sponsor of a worthy TV program and or movie.

5. I support decent movies by attending them.

6. I consider a career in the arts, music, journalism, literature, film and TV to be as important for the kingdom of God as pastoring a church or a mission.

7. I have written at least one letter to the editor of a local paper in the past year.

8. I have read at least one book from the *New York Times* bestseller list in the last year.

9. I am active in civic affairs in my community.

10. I have spoken at least once to a non-believer this month about my relationship with Christ and what it means to be His disciple.

Well, Dinky, how'd you do? If you scored between 8 and 10, then you're a roaring lion; from 5 to 7, you're a semi-viable voice; between 2 and 4, you're just an echo. And watch it – from 0 to 1 – you're a part of the problem instead of the solution.

So, Christian, quit blathering on about how bad it's getting and jump into the battle. Bring a plan and spiritual might with you to help for once. Absolutely refuse the temptation to separate from the culture that God wants us to bless to His honor.

"Each day we are becoming a creature of splendid glory or one of unthinkable horror."

– C.S. Lewis

Chapter 7. Separation: Scriptures' Ultimate Bad Guys

"For those who live in Jerusalem, and their rulers, recognizing neither Him nor the utterances of the prophets which are read every Sabbath, fulfilled these by condemning Him. And though they found no ground for putting Him to death, they asked Pilate that He be executed."

Acts 13:27,28

When the Christian is faced with reaching a wicked culture, he's got three basic options: Absorb it, separate from it or infiltrate it. Let's look at one other aspect of the temptation to separate from society.

Not only does unbiblical separation from the world allow wickedness to continue unchallenged, but it also breeds an "us vs. them" mentality in those who retreat from society. A spiritual xenophobia develops towards the "unsaved, unwashed Gentiles."

Here's the Pharisees' whacked line of reasoning: If worldly environments are evil, and you are godly because you don't hang out at such venues – then those who do frequent such places must be evil. When separation from the world causes the believer to cease interaction with those for whom Christ died to redeem, it is not the separation that God intended in Scripture.

This is the separation that characterized Jesus' favorite group to bash. They were the Scriptures' ultimate bad guys … the piñata of Palestine … you got it – the Pharisees!

The Pharisees, which means "separate ones", wanted to please God. But in their attempts to do so, they separated from anyone or anything that their traditions or their misinterpretation of the law might deem nasty. The Pharisees developed a contemptuous view of others. They thought they were above certain people's levels of depravity, and thus became proud about what they eschewed and what they had achieved. As one minister aptly stated, "Along with their contemptuous view of others, the Pharisees had a shallow sense of forgiveness, a wrong sense of grace and fairness and an unhealthy view of people's failures."

The Pharisees held to the letter of the law, but were blind to the Spirit of the Law and they had no idea how far off base they were. They separated themselves from environments and people to become pleasing in God's sight – at least that was their intention. This misinterpretation of what the Word said led them to become (hello) the very ones whom God detested.

The Pharisees' self-righteous pursuit of outward piety failed to deal with their inward sins of antipathy, wrath, envy, pride, love of Rolexes, browbeating, trap-setting, character assassinations, word games and death plots. And as St. Paul said, though they "professed to know God, they were detestable, disobedient and unfit for any good deed."

The aspects of the world from which we're to be separated are those that are at the core of this world's passions, namely: the lust of the flesh, the lust of the eyes and the boastful pride of life (1Jn.2:15,16).

The worldliness that I should avoid is more a matter of my heart's desire rather than people and places.

"In practice it undermines the transformation of faith. When Christians concentrate their time and energy on their own separate spheres and their own institutions-whether all-absorbing megachurches, Christian yellow-page businesses, or womb-to-tomb Christian cultural ghettoes-they lose the outward thrusting, transforming power that is at the heart of the gospel. Instead of being 'salt' and 'light' - images of a permeating and penetrating action-Christians and Christian institutions become soft and vulnerable to corruption from within."

– Os Guinness

Chapter 8. Rule #1 - Infiltration: Here's Your Excuse to Act Profane

---

"Behold, I send you out as sheep in the midst of wolves; so be shrewd as serpents and innocent as doves."

— Matthew 10:16

Since absorption and separation are not an option for the believer, what is a Christian to do when faced with a godless culture? The only biblical option for the young believer in this situation is to infiltrate society.

This means we must leave our Lysol-disinfected communities and get into the muck and mire of the real world and live what Martin Luther said was the Christian's duty: a *profane life*.

Martin Luther, the 16th century, Augustinian monk who shook all of Christendom like a bowl of liposuctioned fat, thought that a Christian was worthless until he came to a place of maturity where he could live *profanely*. Now don't turn me off … stay frosty. When Martin Luther used the word "profane", he used it in its purest form, which in Latin translates, "outside the temple."

The reason Luther screamed for the Christian to get out of the church and into the world with Christ's gospel was because the ecclesiastical corruption of his time made tradition a usurper of truth, *and* it also removed God and the good news from the common man and the very society the gospel was sent to redeem and conform to God's holy word. Oops.

The Church is also called to be *secular* and *worldly*. The ancient church ordained ministers to a secular priesthood, one that would bring the Scriptures and a biblical worldview to people who are outside of the church.

In this sense, Christ was extremely secular and worldly – which is not bad when we understand what these words really mean. *Secular* simply refers to "the time the world and its inhabitants occupy", i.e., the here and now … the time of our existence.

Christ was concerned with the here and now.

Jesus didn't just dreamily talk about heaven, twiddling his thumbs and waiting to die so he could leave this nasty planet. He set up a massive demon-thrashing organism – the Church – so that in his sacrificial absence we could rock Satan's world by taking back the planet that God so loves.

Christ's message was one of earthly revolution and redemption – not retreat. This is His planet, Baby, and its past the time that we, the Church, woke up to this fact.

This world is the site and purpose of His incarnation. God sent Jesus to redeem the world, and He will accomplish this task through His Spirit-filled people who will cooperatively infiltrate it with Him.

Would that be you?

Think about it, young adult. Think about the ground we can take for God's glory if instead of compromising with our culture, or running from society, we spiritually and intellectually infiltrate the kingdoms of this world with His wisdom and with His power.

"Jesus never spoke to two people the same way, and neither should we. Every single person is unique and individual and deserves an approach that respects that uniqueness."

– Os Guinness

Chapter 9. The Bottom-Feeder's Buddy

"The Son of Man came eating and drinking, and they say, 'Behold, a gluttonous man and a drunkard, a friend of tax collectors and sinners!' Yet wisdom is vindicated by her deeds."

Matthew 11:19

What did Jesus have that caused sinners to seek out His company like Winona Ryder does a Walgreens pharmacist?

How did He, the only perfect person to ever schlep this pebble, manage to attract the notoriously imperfect?

Most believers today wouldn't be seen with some of the folks that Christ insisted on hanging out with. Jesus, God in the flesh, didn't stiff-arm sinners. He frequented their ubiquitous watering holes where the hyper-religious wouldn't dream of being seen. Jesus didn't just hang out with His church buddies – He was a "friend of sinners".

In Jesus' day, the term "sinner" was a general word used to describe the local riff-raff … you know, the scummy crowd. Sinners included the immoral, irreligious, irresponsible, sex-driven, party-till-you-drop types … the bottom-feeders of society … the kind of folks with whom most Christians would not want to have their pictures taken.

And here we see the group Christ targeted, the group with whom He spent a significant amount of time – and on purpose.

Jesus went to where the people lived. He invaded their turf and ministered within their environment, and thus He broke down their barriers, confounded their prejudices and came away with some incredible spoils. Christ infiltrated a pagan environment, without compromise, and led multitudes into a relationship with His Father.

It's funny how quickly we believers become self-righteous and judgmental towards unbelievers, as if we didn't or don't still have the same proclivities towards evil as they do.

Presently, the Church's derisive, hate-filled, petty behavior towards those outside our ecclesiastical four walls is doing more to assist Satan than to help God. You know it's true. What has happened to the separation between church and hate?

It's time to break our ministry out of our stained glass environments and get into this world's problems. How long can we continue to tint our windows to the difficulties of culture? Our attitude towards those outside of Christ's body must be one of compassion and outreach, not one of arrogance and isolation.

In addition to Jesus' example, as a young prophet, Daniel also showed us how to do it right. He got involved with one of the most wicked kingdoms known to man, and by God's grace, caused a decadent king and his kingdom to turn to the Lord and away from idolatry.

May God give us that same heart that radically seeks sinners and the major institutions of our world – reclaiming them for Christ and the Father's glory.

"The secret of success is to be ready when your opportunity comes"

– Benjamin Disraeli

Chapter 10. The King Chose Youth

"Then the king ordered Ashpenaz, the chief of his officials, to bring in some of the sons of Israel, including some of the royal family and of the nobles, youths in whom was no defect, who were good-looking, showing intelligence in every branch of wisdom, endowed with understanding and discerning knowledge, and who had ability for serving in the king's court; and he ordered him to teach them the literature and language of the Chaldeans."

Daniel 1:3,4

Isn't it odd that the very vehicle God used to turn Babylon's kingdom around (that would be the youth) is the same vehicle that is given spiritual scraps in the Church nowadays? In most churches, youth aren't taken very seriously.

Under the guise of "care" and "concern" we give our young adults pizza parties, Hello Kitty teachings and bad drama. We hire a cheerleader/babysitter who has no anointing (other than that of being a nice person) and call him or her a "youth pastor".

This is the all-to-usual path taken by the evangelical world today, faced as we are with raising up the leaders of tomorrow.

What a shame.

Most Christian training of our young warriors is both an insult to God and to the intelligence of the youth themselves. In days of yesteryear, the youth learned great catechisms of the Christian faith and became doctrinally astute, at least in seed form, before they could drive the family chariot.

Today, it's miraculous to hear intelligible theological views coming from adults, much less the youth, concerning the simple basics of the faith in which we stand.

The obsession for temporal "success" that permeates the Americanized Church at the beginning of this new millennium is causing our present neglect of seriously training our youth. And this is setting up the future Church to be devastated by the powers of darkness.

The apostate Pastor, obsessing on the temporal

pleasures of the now, using ministry as a conduit to fill his wallet, bolster his ragged, little ego and prop up his Colgate-grinning image is going to be in for a rude awakening at the judgment seat when God hits rewind on this dude's life, and we see the criminal neglect of this generation of young people.

Church, we've got to wake up and serve this generation. We are way behind in the game, and now we're in the 4th quarter. Look guys, if we don't start taking action immediately in focusing on training the next generation, it will take true shepherds the better part of several decades to undo the effects of our apathy.

Young man or woman, joyfully take your life seriously. Go to a Church that serves you up some serious steak that pushes you to excellence. Because just like Daniel and his three amigos … you are the Church's – and our culture's – only hope. You are the primary one whom God chooses.

Now the word of the Lord came to me saying,

"Before I formed you in the womb I knew you,
And before you were born I consecrated you;
I have appointed you a prophet to the nations."

Then I said, "Alas, Lord God!
Behold, I do not know how to speak,
Because I am a youth."

But the Lord said to me,
"Do not say, 'I am a youth,'
Because everywhere I send you, you shall go,
And all that I command you, you shall speak.

"Do not be afraid of them,
For I am with you to deliver you," declares the Lord.

Then the Lord stretched out His hand and touched
my mouth, and the Lord said to me,
"Behold, I have put My words in your mouth.

"See, I have appointed you this day over the na-
tions and over the kingdoms,
To pluck up and to break down,
To destroy and to overthrow,
To build and to plant."

– Jeremiah 1:4-10

Chapter 11. The History of Heroes is the History of Youth

"Let no one look down on your youthfulness, but rather in speech, conduct, love, faith and purity, show yourself an example of those who believe."

1st Timothy 4:12

Young Christian Adult, do you realize that no matter how neglected and confused you may feel, you are the key, under the discipline of the Holy Spirit, to turn this *Titanic* of a nation around before it hits the proverbial iceberg?

The prophet Joel said it is the young men and women who will have the visions that will constructively shape our future.

That's you, Dude.

Don't think that God will never use you just because you're young. Throughout Scripture and history, youth have had an incredible influence on our
society. The Scripture is replete with examples of
God using – and in dramatic fashion – young men
and women.

You know, when most of us think about the type
of person God uses, we usually think of some old cat
sporting a gray beard, wearing little eyeglasses with
a scowl on his face carting around a Bible that's big-
ger than Rebel Wilson's boxers. We forget that Jesus Himself started his ministry when He was thirty
years old and was finished at the ripe old age of thir-
ty-three. Check out this short list of young "greats"
found in the Scripture and in Church history, and let
this motivate you to seek God in order for Him to use
you in like manner.

- John the Baptist was a little over the 30-
  mark when he rocked all of Israel.

- David was a youth when he slew Goliath.
  When God sought for a man to eternally
  shut Goliath's pie hole, he found a youth
  who acted like a man.

- Solomon became king over Israel at an
  early age, and God gave this young king
  wisdom that blew away his elders.

- Jeremiah, as a youth, was called as a prophet to the nations – to uproot, destroy, build and plant them according to the word of God.

- Charles Spurgeon was only nineteen when he began his acclaimed pastorate in England.

- John Calvin, at twenty-seven years of age, wrote his world-reforming *Institutes,* which has profoundly impacted theological and political thought.

As Benjamin Disraeli said, "The history of heroes is the history of youth." God has a high view of youth. It's not because they are cute, but because they are spiritually lethal. They are the warriors that God uses to cut a swath through the demonic bondages that hold men captive. Their zeal is proverbial … and when it is mixed with divine wisdom, they are a severe threat to Satan and his defeated ilk.

All the aforementioned young adults were forces, and he that is destined to be a force will be put on his mettle at an early age.

So get with it, young adult. Quit being a slacker … get a vision … get on your face … and get ready for God to make you the next giant-slayer.

PART THREE:

More Biblical Disciplines for Influential Believers

"If you want a religion to make you feel really comfortable, I certainly don't recommend Christianity."

– C.S. Lewis

Chapter 12. Rule #2:
Deal with Your Defects.

"The King chose youth in whom was no defect..."

The world, though antagonistic, will acknowledge our good works and glorify God – at least according to the Bible, they will. Arrogant, slimy and wicked, King Nebuchadnezzar looked among God's youth to find credible servants to work in his courts. He found four.

I believe society is going to get so screwed up by atheistic philosophies, by crooked politicians and by inter-galactic family problems that the world is finally going to turn to the church for help and direction.

The question is, will we be able to offer it?

Moreover, are we prepared to step up to the plate and actually *deliver* the assistance once we offer it?

Do we have a blueprint for society that isn't religiously naïve, narrow and culturally unviable?

In order to assure your rise to a place of godly influence, you must begin now to deal with your defects.

Check it out: Salvation isn't the end of God's dealings with you; it's just the beginning. Neither is your Christian life to be one of never-ending Christian boy-band concerts and covered-dish dinners. God has elected us to bring healing to the nations, but He'll never deploy us to a full extent until we have met His standards of excellence.

So, let's go to work on our deficiencies – our defects. Then, when the time comes, we'll be ready.

All of us are defective in some form or fashion. There's not a sound bone in our bodies outside of Christ. We're radically corrupt. That's why, without Him, we're toast. Yet, when Christ regenerates us, He gives us the gift of faith that, according to Scripture, can radically make us strong where before we were weak.

God's grace and our faith not only secure for us eternal redemption, but also the power to create temporal and massively transforming change. God delights in taking people that society overlooks and equipping them in a tremendous way, but He doesn't get glory and great use out of these people by just snapping His fingers over their heads.

If you're one of these people (and I'm willing to bet if you bought this book, you are), He's going to put you through the spiritual wringer. At times, you're going to think He doesn't like you too much. That's why Scripture has to state over and over again that when God begins the process of spiritual discipline, you need to hang on tight and remember that He loves you. Because when you're being processed, it feels like anything but the love of God.

God, who chooses the weak and ignoble, has epic and noble goals that He wants you to accomplish – goals that, in and of yourself, you can't accomplish. Therefore, you've got to realize that in order to get to that place of effectiveness, you must go through serious training ... training along the lines of an Olympic athlete or Marine. And even though He accepts you in your defective state, He loves you too much to let you remain in that state. His discipline is going to deal with your shortcomings so that you can rule in your own "Babylon".

Becoming an asset to Christ in the earth is part of the Father's ultimate end in laying hold of you. Sure, He chose you because of His great love for you; but

He also chose you for a vocation (not a vacation) so you can do your part in His eternal purpose of discipling nations.

Nowadays, you hear believers compared to all sorts of things: sheep, orphans, lost coins, babes, sons, daughters, brides ... But seldom do you hear the believer made analogous to an athlete or a soldier. I would venture a thousand to one that you usually hear the believer likened to that which is passive versus that which is highly disciplined.

Satan, though defeated, is anything but stupid, and he had to do something to level the battlefield. So he got several blind pastors to remove from the body of Christ all the teachings that emphasize spiritual discipline and a hearty engagement of culture. The devil got us focused on playing games in a sort of Christian Disneyland, drowning us in endless soulish and erotic 'Christian' songs, peddling Christian clichés to a simple beat that any clunk can dance to. He's clouded the fact that we're called to be soldiers in God's army that is currently engaged in a war against – not other people – but demonic strongholds that possess nations.

Satan has effectively taken from the church the understanding that we're running a race and fighting a battle of eternal consequences that demands that we buffet all of our spiritual defects.

The young prophet Daniel and his three buddies were of great use to God in a wicked kingdom for many reasons, one being that they were without defect. Although these defects speak of physical deformities, we must take seriously and crucify all spiritual deformities of immaturity and unrepentant sin if we are serious about influencing our culture for His name's sake.

Clean shirt, new shoes
And I don't know where I am goin' to
Silk suit, black tie,
I don't need a reason why
They come runnin' just as fast as they can
'Cause every girl crazy 'bout a sharp
dressed man.

– ZZ Top

Chapter 13. Rule #3: Sharp Dressed Man.

"The King chose youths who were good-looking…"

In the days of Daniel the prophet, King Nebuchadnezzar wouldn't allow anyone who was not good-looking to serve in his court.

What can we as modern day Christians learn from this Old Testament passage with regard to influencing our present-day "Babylon" as Daniel did the one of old? The lesson is clear: It's "Hey Christian… Shape it up." and, as carnal as it may sound, "Pay attention to how you look."

Now, I'm not talking about redemption based on looks, but an effective use of our appearances in the world that Christ has commanded us to disciple. Sure, God loves you, Stinky … just as you are.

But if you're going to influence society for Christ, you're going to have to bathe, wear deodorant, clip your braidable nose hair, tuck in your shirttail, get a haircut, wear matching socks ... and a little cologne wouldn't hurt.

The Bible states that God looks on the heart, but man looks on the outward appearance; therefore, the Church needs to realize that the people we're attempting to reach are judging us *immediately* based on how we appear outwardly.

I hate to seem negative, but Christians, for the most part, are a poor-looking batch of people, living either on the extreme poles of the shabby legalist or the ostentatious and gaudy charismatic *nouveau riche.* Some believers are seemingly always living on the lunatic fringe of taste, style and decorum, spooking unbelievers simply because of the odd way they appear.

You know, there's a silly notion in the body of Christ that the worse you look, the more holy you are. Well, if that is true, then most of the Church is holy, holy, holy. By the way – I don't accept that idea for one minute.

True separation and holiness should make you look better rather than worse. When Daniel separated inwardly from Babylon's idolatry, he looked ten times better, not ten times worse.

Now, let's clarify what I'm talking about in regard to looking your best. I'm well aware of the different body types ... that some of you are ectos, some are endos and mesos; and there's really nothing that can be done about your skeletal structure. And I couldn't care less what's currently *en vogue* with *Cosmo* or *GQ*.

What I'm advocating is taking care of your body so that, in case you have to walk a long way across the parking lot to get to church on Sunday morning, you're not wheezing and near heart attack-status requiring the deacons to keep the defibrillator juiced up and ready to jump start your heart just to keep you alive for praise and worship.

I'm also advocating presenting yourself to those around you in such a manner that they are drawn to you, rather than repulsed by you. If you're too shabby or too gaudy, people won't take you seriously, much less the Christ you preach.

Let's look our best because we represent the King of Kings.

In case you're not getting it, I'll be more specific. Christians should create and assume a sense of style and taste to look their best and get the most out of their appearance. Ugliness is *not* holiness.

It *does* matter what we look like, because we're dealing with a society that looks on the outward appearance; and in the world – you never have a second chance to make a first impression.

Looking great isn't difficult. There are some simple secrets to looking your best (and don't skip over this like it's carnal stuff). Don't kid yourself that all that matters is 'being filled with the Holy Ghost and fire.'

The Holy Ghost made certain that it was noted in Scripture that one of the reasons why Daniel and his compadres were chosen to serve in the king's court was because they looked good. Their looks were among the many qualities that earned them a pretty exciting life of serving God.

You might not want to admit it, but the fact remains that if you look well, you get treated better. People in the church have spent that last, oh, 2,000 years working on the inner man and not really very long working on the issues of how they appear outwardly to the world. If we don't think looks matter in this culture, then we are truly a few fries short of a Happy Meal. What's more, if we don't think the

Holy Spirit's work on our inner man leads to the cleaning up of the outer man – we need to drink a double espresso and wake the heck up.

Unclean, unkempt and unfit screams, "I'm undisciplined. I'm outta control. I'm unbalanced." The believer should have order and excellence over his spirit, mind *and* body. God works on the complete package. There is nothing freaky, shocking or incongruent about the practical aspects of having God, whose very name is excellent, express His life through us in an excellent fashion.

We need to realize that our personal presentation – body, face (that includes your demeanor – smile every once in a while), haircut, clothes – are a backdrop to who we are. They are not *who* we are; but they help set the stage for us and for everything we say and do.

The mature Christian will communicate stability, strength, elegance, intelligence and confidence through his personal presentation by looking sharp, solid and smart. Watch what happens when you take your time to look your best.

Stupid girl
(Woo)
Stupid girls
Stupid girls
Maybe if I act like that
That guy will call me back
Porno paparazzi girls (yeah)
I don't wanna be a stupid girl (uh-huh)

– Pink

Chapter 14. Rule #4: Intelligence in Every Branch of Wisdom

"The King chose youths showing intelligence in every branch of wisdom..."

Daniel and his friends were chosen by Nebuchadnezzar, not only because of God's sovereignty in steering the heart of the king to choose them, but also because -- under God's hand – they developed their minds to a place where they were intelligent in every branch of wisdom.

It wasn't enough that they were "filled with the Holy Ghost and fire."

It wasn't enough that God loved them and "had a wonderful plan for their life."

It wasn't enough that they had Christian bumper stickers, listened to Christian music and were still virgins.

That's fine ... that's cool. But in order for them to impact an aggressively godless culture, they had to bring well-developed brains to the table – not just sweetness and personal virtues. The king wanted, and God promoted, young adults "who showed intelligence in every branch of wisdom."

There are a couple of points regarding anti-intellectualism that I really want to pound into you, the young adult, so that you won't perpetuate the same blights that we, your predecessors, have. Catch these two points, act on them, and you'll automatically become a player in the development of your society.

Are you ready?

First of all, realize that Evangelical anti-intellectualism is a *scandal*. It is a scandal in the sense of being, as Os Guinness said, "an offense and a stumbling block that needlessly hinders people from considering the Christian faith and coming to Christ." Sometimes when I see Christians on TV attempting to give a reasonable and logical answer to a legitimate question shot at them by an unbeliever, I want to tear the fish symbol off my car.

Those who purport to know the all-knowing, all-wise God, who gives to the believer the mind of Christ, the gifts of the word of wisdom and the word of knowledge, should not be giving abecedarian answers couched in indecipherable religious argot.

We should be the sharpest, most reasonable, rational and easy to understand folks on the planet. Why? Because the God we're supposedly plugged into *is*. Guys, we really must shape up our *Jell-O* pudding brains. No joke – it is scandalous for us to be stupid.

To remain anti-intellectual is to keep people from coming to Christ.

It is insulting to God and man.

It is courting failure.

It is ensuring the relegation of the Church to the back of the short bus.

Secondly, anti-intellectualism is a *sin*. It is a sin because it is a refusal, contrary to the first of Jesus' two great commandments, to love the Lord your God with your mind, as well as your heart and soul and strength.

As Ambassador Charles Malik warned in his incisive address at the dedication of the Billy Graham

Center at Wheaton College in 1980, speaking as an Orthodox believer to Evangelicals: "I must be frank with you: the greatest danger besetting American Evangelical Christianity is the danger of Anti-intellectualism. The mind, as to its greatest and deepest riches, is not cared for enough."

God commands us to love Him with all of our minds. This is a commandment – not a suggestion. He didn't just slap that rule on those who wanted to enter seminary. Every Christian is to love Him with all of his or her mind. Some people have a greater intellectual capacity than others, and God's not asking you to be like your buddy who was *magna cum laude*. He's simply asking you to do all you can do – because all you can do is all you can do, and all you can do is enough.

If you can look God, your fellow believers and your unsaved buddies in the eye and honestly say that you love Him with your entire mind – then chill out. But most Christians couldn't look a Cyclops in the eye and honestly say that they are obeying the vastness of that command. What an awesome rule: *Love Him with all your mind...*

Loving God with our minds is not a question of orthodoxy or intellect, but of love. How many times have we heard, "If you really loved God, you wouldn't be having premarital sex?" Okay, that's a no-groiner. Or, "If you really loved God, you wouldn't get drunk and drive your truck into the convenience store and steal cigarettes?" All right, these are simple, undeniable wrongs that have to be crucified.

But compared to the list of vices that we ordinarily acknowledge, we seldom hear our brother's keeper convicting us for being stupid or foolish. "Thou shalt not drink beer" isn't one of the great commandments, and neither is "Thou shalt not watch a PG-13 movie." These aren't the burning issues on God's heart.

What He's impassioned about is your loving Him with all your heart, soul, strength, and *MIND*.

Anti-intellectualism is a scandal and a sin.

So what do we do?

Glad you asked.

Here's a simple can-do:

First, examine your ignorance and confess that it's pervasive. Note all of the things that govern our world, and then figure out which of those things you don't happen to have a clue about. Now go get the skinny on them.

Define them; learn their constituent parts and how they work. If you are going to be a real influence in your world for Christ, you need to be in the know. This is the information age … it's all at your fingertips. It's all out there for the knowing. It's easy. But, that which is easy to do is also easy *not* to do.

So do it.

Secondly, repent of your stupidity. Realize it and turn from this wickedness. If this is a *great* commandment – then to break it is a *great* sin. Start seeing foolishness and stupidity as rebellion.

This is not a light thing. Don't trivialize it. Don't vilify the obviously profane while you remain ignorant. You're just as bad in God's eyes. It's sin that demands repentance. It is something you can change.

Don't worry if people ridicule you for studying too much. They ridiculed Paul: "Your great learning has driven you mad." Don't worry about what critics will say of you for joyfully taking life seriously – we are here to change our world. That's a massive job that will be accomplished only by the fittest.

So, get into intellectual shape! You can be sure that just as Daniel and his three sidekicks ascended to a place of influence in a wicked kingdom because they showed intelligence in every branch of wisdom, so you will position yourself for dominion in your sphere of influence.

"If you're like most people, you probably seek first to be understood; you want to get your point across. And in doing so, you may ignore the other person completely, pretend that you're listening, selectively hear only certain parts of the conversation or attentively focus on only the words being said, but miss the meaning entirely. So why does this happen? Because most people listen with the intent to reply, not to understand."

– Stephen Covey

Chapter 15. Rule #5: In All Your Getting, Get Understanding

"The King chose youths endowed with understanding…"

The Christian cannot afford *not* to understand what is happening in this world – be it in the church, politics, education, business, media, or the arts. His lack of understanding leads to a lack of involvement that relegates the church to be the back of the godless bus. Get it right, Christian, this ain't the happy bus.

This bus is driven by a drunk George Soros with Isaac Asimov riding shotgun, heading toward a brick wall. And what's more – there are no airbags, no seat belts, and the speedometer is buried at 185 mph.

Can you feel it?

I hate to sound like the Grinch, but the Church

is in deep weeds, folks, and this nation is going to be more lost than Bella Thorne sitting in on a Ravi Zacharias roundtable unless we become like the sons of Issachar, who "understood the times." We must become fully aware of what we are dealing with as a nation and what each of us should be doing as the people of God. Our nation's hope is based upon the Church rising to the occasion, rather than fleeing the scene of this "accident".

God powerfully used Daniel because he understood what was happening in Babylon. Daniel's knowledge and understanding were not limited to what was happening in the church, to who was topping the contemporary Christian music charts or to knowing who *Charisma* magazine's Playmate of the month was.

Daniel was a young man of understanding who grasped the prevailing winds that blew his nation onto the rocks of idolatry and wickedness. If the church wants to be involved with steering our nation back to God and returning to righteousness, it's going to require a little more homework than what we are used to doing.

The topics of understanding must expand beyond the current pop Christian subculture to the philosophical undercurrents that have caused our society to drift radically off course.

Also, every young believer must understand the components of the Christian worldview contained in the scripture if we want to cease standing intellectually naked before Secular Humanism, Communism and bizarre Islamic extremism.

Within the rebellious and morally bankrupt milieu of secular higher education, the Christian worldview – and our boldness to proclaim it – must stand out like Mike Pence at a Nelly concert.

The importance of understanding the Christian Worldview as laid out in Scripture cannot be overstated. It is a must if we want to pull our motherland out of Satan's hands and back into the redeeming arms of God.

Young Christian, unless you are intellectually equipped to offensively defend the Christian worldview over and against the Humanists, Communists, Muslims and the *weltanschauung* of the radical Left that's fired at you in the college classroom (not to mention the majority of your online intake on a 24/7 basis) – you are toast.

Christian parents are terrified nowadays of sending their biblically raised offspring to a state-run university: Fear of their babies' showing up on YouTube naked; being involved in a beer guzzling frat party; dating Skeeter, the dorm's dope dealer; running into a Ted Bundy wannabe or dropping acid at a party … these are minute phobias compared to the Jurassic-sized panic of a systematic, daily de-construction of everything they have attempted to teach their kids over the previous 18 years.

After spending the best years of their lives and tens (if not hundreds) of thousands of dollars raising their kids, parents are watching their precious investment go down the crapper when their children set foot in the university. By the end of the first week of freshman orientation, everything that has to do with Christianity is immediately trashed like a picture of Trump at Hillary's house.

Welcome to the 21st century, Christian … May I take your coat?

Do you need more bad news? You do? Ok. Here you go. Family values are shot down in the co-ed dorms where the only place there is more premarital sex is on Saturday nights at Russell Brand's Mansion. Condoms are distributed like Tic-Tacs after an all-you-can-eat sardine and Gorgonzola cheese dinner. As for your religious views, biblical theism isn't even on the platform. It is replaced by atheism, agnosticism and nihilism, while social values are replaced by radical politics, socialism, Islam and Fidel.

Upon entrance to the campus, the believer is barraged with safe-sex kits, trial marriage arrangements and feminist agendas. Pro-homosexual materials are passed out in the breezeway by Timmy & Tommy, the transgendered twins, and the Christian viewpoint is more abused and scorned than Harvey Weinstein at a viewing of *Sense and Sensibility.*

So what's the believer to do? Run? Hide? Give up?

I don't think so. No, indeed, the young adult is called to reclaim the classroom, the public square – yes, and the Church – for the glory of God.

The Biblical Christian worldview forms the basis for such a venture; therefore, it's a must to study, understand and apply. This line of action will arm young Christian men and women regarding the various intellectual battlefields and enemies set against them during their academic years, as well as equip them for productive and Christ-centered lives.

Since I've been prattling on about understanding the Biblical Christian Worldview, as well as that of the Secular Humanists, Muslims, Marxist-Leninists, I thought I might define the heart of a worldview using David Noebel's definition in his excellent work,

Understanding the Times:

> The term worldview refers to any ideology, phi-
> losophy, theology, movement or religion that
> provides an overarching approach to understand-
> ing God, the world and man's relations to God
> and the world. Specifically, a worldview should
> contain a particular perspective regarding each
> of the following ten disciplines: theology, phi-
> losophy, ethics, biology, psychology, sociology,
> law, politics, economics and history. If Biblical
> Christianity contains a specific attitude toward all
> ten disciplines, it is by our definition, a world-
> view. And, since it contains a theology, it is by
> implication a religious worldview. Secular Hu-
> manism and Marxism-Leninism are also reli-
> gious ... both have theologies. Further, both are
> worldviews, because they speak directly to each
> of the nine other disciplines. The New Age move-
> ment (Cosmic Humanism), on the other hand, is
> an emerging worldview, because it has something
> to say about some of the categories (e.g., law and
> sociology). Each worldview offers a particular
> perspective from which to approach each disci-
> pline. Conversely, each discipline is value laden
> with worldview implications. Christian students
> must understand that these various disciplines are
> not value free. Each discipline demands basic as-
> sumptions about the nature of reality in order to
> grant meaning to specific approaches to it.

By further in-depth study of these topics, the
Christian will begin to understand, finally, strange

cats like Anderson Cooper, Alec Baldwin, Joy Behar, Anjem Choudary, Hillary Clinton, left wing politics and politicians, CNN, and ultimately, why their state-run universities crank out such bizarre lemmings.

Lastly, and importantly, if young believers are intelligent and have a high moral threshold, they must tether their hearts to fallen humanity with equal amounts of empathy. Otherwise, they will become arrogant and unable to relate to those who haven't reached their level of sainthood, and thereby sever the lines of communication.

Even though Daniel and his mates radically opposed Babylon and its way of life, they didn't come across like self-righteous choirboys. That's kind of important, if you want to have non-Christians listen to you and subsequently affect a biblical change.

Endowed with an understanding of the Babylonians' philosophical persuasions and proclivities to sin, Daniel successfully communicated God's truth in a thoughtful manner and thus swayed a very naughty ruler into the paths of righteousness.

Behold: the power of not being a religious jerk in our defense of truth.

Think about it. Daniel knew he was right. He knew he had the answers to the king's nightmares.

He knew Babylon was in deep yogurt and needed his godly help. But he didn't become an ass about it. Daniel didn't become a hate-filled, derisive, condescending goose-stepper regarding his wisdom, his ethical standards and Nebuchadnezzar's lack of holiness.

As much as Christians are to challenge Babylon's actions and ideologies, we must be considerate and gracious, not self-righteous and thus repulsive. No one wants to listen to a know-it-all. No one wants to listen to a living heart donor. Especially some undergrad who grew up in Church and has spent his first twenty-one years in an amniotic *Kool-Aid*-filled sack with no clue about the difficulties and intricacies of being estranged from God in an atheistic world.

It's obviously a must that the believer is to engage our culture with biblical solutions for modern problems. Equally important is the manner in which we do it. We can radically and fundamentally disagree with our society and still be gracious and sympathetic toward a fallen world with which we're at odds.

Since we're called to be in Babylon's face, let's make sure we do it with grace. In your face with grace. We must avoid the pompous attitude that is often present in being right. As we work to change our own "Babylon", we must truly seek first to understand the Babylonians before we try to make ourselves understood, realizing that our job is not just to be right, but to be a viable minister of reconciliation to a wicked world that God so loves.

"Creative persuasion is a matter of being biblical, not of being either modern or postmodern."

– Os Guinness

Chapter 16. Rule #6:
Discern Knowledge

"The King chose youths who with discerning knowledge…"

Daniel and his buddies were not just Jewish, teenage, role models of goodness and propriety. They were young men who walked with God and understood how to use their spiritual gifts, in particular, the gift of wisdom, the gift of discernment and the word of knowledge.

In dealing with righting a radically wrong kingdom, Daniel and his rowdies needed supernatural knowledge and discernment – or their heads would roll. Nebuchadnezzar was in no mood for guestimates regarding his Babylon's dilemmas. Babylon would listen to Daniel if, and only if, Daniel struck the mark. If not, the king would make mince meat out of him. And did he ever try.

The stakes were high – it's not as if Daniel's ministry was within the safe and patient walls of a sweet community Church with an understanding pastor to make allowances for Daniel's mistakes when exercising his wisdom gifts. Babylon's tolerance level for error were nil; therefore, and of necessity, Daniel's wise counsel had to be right on the money. No mistakes. No errors. It was time for the men to step forth and for the boys to go home.

So it is now.

The culture we've been given to reach in the Western world is nightmarish, and we, like Daniel, must have the ability to answer our societal bad dream with what God *is* saying. We must respond with the godly remedy to our situation and stay the wrathful hand of the God whose patience we have exhausted.

Daniel knew that to reach a wicked kingdom for Jehovah, he must answer its questions and bring a strategy that all of Satan's ilk could neither access nor fathom. Therefore, within that God-intolerant environment, it wasn't tongues that were the hottest and most important gift, and it wasn't the gift of miracles. It was the "wisdom" gifts – the gift of wisdom, the gift of discernment and the word of knowledge. These were what moved Daniel into the king's court with God's answers to their problems.

Look, Christian – without the supernatural gifts of wisdom, discernment and knowledge in our lives – we're just Boy Scouts who mean well in a bad nation.

So, how do we move in the gifts of wisdom, discernment and knowledge?

Well, first of all we've got to hangout with God. Why? Because the wisdom gifts differ from common sense and natural wisdom (though they don't necessarily contradict) in that God lets you in on special revelation of your situation by dropping in your spirit information for the task at hand.

With these gifts, God imparts facts and info that are difficult to know. Even though receiving this information is a gift and not a work of our own doing, it clearly demands devoting ourselves to serious prayer, meditation and Bible reading, thus creating a sensitivity to the Holy Spirit, His ways, His wisdom and His timing.

In other words, it's going to take a concentrated effort on our part, cooperating with the Holy Spirit and earnestly desiring these spiritual gifts before they become an integral part of our spiritual makeup.

You may be an ambassador to England or France
You may like to gamble, you might like to dance
You may be the heavyweight champion of the world
You may be a socialite with a long string of pearls
But you're gonna have to serve somebody, yes
Indeed you're gonna have to serve somebody
Well, it may be the devil or it may be the Lord
But you're gonna have to serve somebody

– Bob Dylan

Chapter 17. Rule #7:
You Gotta Serve Somebody

"The King chose youth who had ability for serving…"

Popular in some western evangelical circles is phraseology regarding "taking dominion" over a city, region or – what the heck – why not the planet? This, admittedly, sounds better than what the defeatist branches of Christendom preach, namely that "Satan is alive and well … the antichrist is coming … it's all going to hell!"

What troubles me in this victorious clarion call of "taking dominion" is how it smacks of selfishness and entitlement, not of practical servanthood – blood, sweat and tears poured out for a godless society. If there is anything that the western Church wants (in particular, America's aberrant version), it is something for nothing and our checks for free.

We want dominion. We want authority. We want power – but *without* paying the price of serving and of saving sinners and a twisted culture. The authority that the Church is to exert in the earth is not magisterial, but ministerial. We aren't kings to whom the world should cater, but priests who have been appointed to serve men in the things that pertain unto God. So put down your crown's polishing cloth and pick up that bath towel and get ready to wash some dirty feet … okay, Felicia?

The Gospel's way is not via *taking* dominion, rather, *serving* your way to a place of recognition. You know the unsaved world has had enough of derisive, hate-filled protests and marches by religious extremists who put very little into the community except cacophonic, unbalanced screeching about what is wrong, instead of being loving, living examples of what is right.

We forget so often in our denunciation of wickedness that Christ actually served and wept for wicked people. He nurtured the naughty, prospered the pariahs and assisted the slimy, and though this freaked out the religious community – it riveted the sinners' attention.

What is this?

The pure, sinless, holy Son of God actually serving the rugrats he created? Yeah, and he didn't do it just to seem different; he did it in order to kill the sinner with kindness. He was showing fallen man that the pagans who deserved hell could instead be nurtured by the Ultimate Judge, who came not to condemn men, but to save their souls and help them in their practical needs.

If, as young adults, you begin serving our community in its most critical areas of need, then one day, after 20 years of solid service and getting your hands dirty in our city's problems, your servant spirits will bring you before the pillars of the community.

If you don't believe me, just get Tyler Henry to ask Billy Graham.

"If you know the enemy and know yourself, you need not fear the result of a hundred battles. If you know yourself but not the enemy, for every victory gained you will also suffer a defeat. If you know neither the enemy nor yourself, you will succumb in every battle."

– Sun Tzu

Chapter 18. Rule #8.
Learning the Literature and Language of Your Culture

"The king chose youth who learned the literature and language of the Chaldeans…"

One of the reasons why Daniel and his bros led in Babylon was because they knew the literature and the language of the Babylonians.

They read … then led.

Imagine that?

Unfortunately, reading among young adults is about as popular as LeBron James showing up at a David Duke's family reunion wearing a Malcolm-X t-shirt and discussing the outrageous lack of African Americans winning Oscars.

Only readers become leaders.

One of the reasons why we don't read is because, thanks to modern media, we have developed the attention span of a ferret on double café mocha. If something doesn't scratch our itch, stroke our soft underbelly, arouse us immediately or quickly solve a long-term problem *and* do it in stereo surround sound ... well, then, the heck with it! It's time to move on to the next buzz.

The Christian often relies too heavily on 'social media' or Netflix for diversionary info and enjoyment instead of reading. But if we want to change our world, we're going to have to take a tip from the *Cable Guy*: kill that babysitter and then pick up a good book.

I personally loathe the menial level of my past literary intake. Prodigious I was not. Spending twenty-one years skating through school trying to read as little as possible because Pink Floyd told me, "We don't need no education," left me working at a gas station, smoking weed and one audition away from the lead role in *Dumb & Dumber.*

Christ had to drag me into His kingdom in order to change my view of education. His pulling me out of the miry clay not only freed me from serious iniquity, but also gave me a desire and a reason to shape up the silly putty between my ears.

Having said that, let's now look at what we can do about our big-time stupidity.

First of all, build a library.

Every Christian needs a killer library covering a wide variety of topics. Don't just read the things your own denomination or non-denomination peddles. You'll get warped if you feed solely within an insular environment. Here are some basic categories to get you started:

The Bible. Get one and – as odd as this sounds – read it. From stem to stern. It doesn't help you to have it on your night stand. It's not a lucky charm, even though it is magically delicious. Read it in as many versions as possible. Make it your book of books.

Study Aids. I recommend actually purchasing a concordance, a lexicon, a standard dictionary, a thesaurus, an exhaustive Scripture reference guide, a Bible dictionary and a Webster's 1828 dictionary. The reason being? Well, I'm old and I like actual books I can hold and write in, that's 'why'. Sure, you'll be out a little cash – but you're going to use them for the rest of your life.

Changing the world is a costly venture. So pay the price. That said, if you're more of an online person, then as you well know, the world is your oyster when it comes to having access to excellent info.

Theology. The other day I heard this guy say, "I don't like theology …I just love Jesus." I replied in my usual first-Corinthians-thirteen manner: "Excuse me, Mr. Bodine, but what turnip wagon did you fall off of, and which wheel ran you over?"

The fact of the matter is, you can't love God if you don't know Him *biblically*. The study of theology is not just a matter of orthodoxy, but one of love. Every Christian is a theologian – either a good one or a bad one.

For God's sake, your sake, the Church's sake and the unbeliever's sake – study the Word. Study in order to make you wise unto salvation, but also to make you effective and powerful in explaining it to others – both sinners and saints, both the learned and the supermodels.

Take your faith seriously.

Biographies. Read about the lives of great men and women of God who had powerful ministries, influenced godly political change, fought for human rights, fed the poor and sacrificed everything to reach men for the glory of Christ. Read about their struggles, their failures and their triumphs. Then follow those good ole' shampoo instructions: lather, rinse and repeat … Apply their actions and faith and attitudes in the situation to which God has presently called you.

Books on the Martyrs. Here's some unnerving reading: the cost that a few brave hearts paid to advance the Gospel. Reading about the martyrs gives the believer an historical object lesson of the people who actually believed the Gospel and lived it out to the point that it cost them their lives. In addition to this, it gives great perspective to our problems, revealing that the great majority of what we are going through is tremendously inconsequential … a mere molehill in the Garden of Eden.

The martyrs will shake you to the core and jerk any grumbling, complaining and lukewarm slack out of your spiritual life.

Philosophy and Philosophers. Most folks who major in philosophy in college usually end up tending bar at Chili's. Philosophy is seen by the average American to be about as useful in "real life" as a crappy gun in mud. Nevertheless, this discipline (even if it doesn't seem like an urgent imperative to know and understand) affects not only the way we think, but, just as importantly, the way we live.

Philosophy takes a closer look at the ideas behind how we live our lives. What we believer to be true affects our view of ourselves, how we treat other humans and the world in which we live. Though it doesn't seem like there is a lot of thought involved in social media, most conversations, TV, politics and educational policy – be assured, these all stem from a system of thought. As believers, we must recognize these thought systems in order to first deconstruct the destructive components in them that lead to the demise of our culture and then reconstruct a more excellent way according to God's wisdom.

Studying philosophy is a must, as it helps the young Christian to recognize what is really being said, where the ideas come from and where they are going to lead.

History. Those who don't learn from the past are doomed to repeat it. If you don't believe me, just ask Taylor Swift.

There is much to be learned by pausing to look backward and then chilling out and thinking about what has transpired up until now. When one studies history, one quickly begins to see the prosperity of nations that honored God and the dissolution of those who turned their backs on Him. Studying our past gives us discernment for our present decisions and wisdom in our plans for tomorrow.

The Classics. Because today's youth have the concentration level of a whitetail deer on crystal meth, a working vocabulary below that of Snoop Dog's Macaw, the passion of Britney Spears wanting to answer the ultimate life questions of life, and a total IQ less than the front row of a Bruno Mars concert – the Classics today stand even more neglected than Rosie's *8 Minute Abs* download.

According to Os Guinness, when most people think of a "classic" today, they don't think of a book, but a Coke, or a 1950s roadster, or perhaps an early Beatles' song. Mark Twain defined the problem: a classic is a book that people praise, but don't read.

Why is it necessary for young adults to read the classics? Shouldn't only the dorks wearing flood pants read this stuff, while Christians spend our time loitering at Starbucks and listening to transexuals on iTunes?

Huh?

According to Dr. Louise Cowan, we all are to read great books because,

They have been found to enhance and elevate the consciousness of all sorts of people who study them, to lift their readers out of narrowness or provincialism into a wider vision of humanity. Further, they guard the truths of the human heart from faddish half-truths of the day by straightening the mind and imagination and enabling their readers to judge for themselves. In a word, they lead those who will follow into a perception of the fullness and the complexity of reality.

Within a society that screams for us to pay attention to the minutiae and the immediate, foregoing contemplation upon the eternal and consequential, if the young adult doesn't want to be generational carnage, he must read things that are weighty, timeless, inspiring and instructional.

As C.S. Lewis wrote:

"We all, therefore, need the books that will correct the characteristic mistakes of our own period. And that means the old books ... the only palliative is to keep the clean sea breeze of the centuries blowing through our minds, and this can be done only by reading old books. It is a good rule, after reading a new book, never to allow yourself another new one till you have read an old one in between. If that is too much for you, you should at least read one old one to every three new ones."

Pop Culture (literature, music, art, video, movies, TV and poetry). Here's where the majority of Christians bite it in their cultural intake. Shallow as it may sound, not keeping up with modern society can be a real detriment to your usefulness to God. Daniel and the boys lived in a society that caused them to undergo more changes than Bruce Jenner during menopause, and amazingly, with each cultural shift, they stayed on top of the board and rode each wave.

If we are going to reach the society that Christ has given us to alter, it will demand our staying on top of what those who influence our mission field are saying and doing. This means, as a missionary, reading the contemporary stuff, watching TV, videos, movies and listening to music. But don't just listen mindlessly – listen as an analyst dissecting the beliefs and values of these temporary icons, as well as their effects upon their audiences and the Christian worldview. This will help us to communicate the Gospel in the context of our day ... not of the Von Trapp's.

One of the keys to reaching anyone with anything is to understand where they are and where they have come from spiritually, intellectually and culturally. Living in a modern world, we can't be monkish in our avoidance of the multifaceted influences that affect the culture in which we've been sovereignly placed.

Therefore, as you watch an estimated 50 hours a week of programs – between the giggles, your sixteenth bag of Lays and your fifth Coke – pause to listen and maybe even scratch down some casual observations made during an episode of the various chum-slicks you view.

Simply increasing your sensitivity to what you are actually seeing and hearing will serve tremendously in making your message alive with current illustrations couched in a Gospel context. Epoxying the twain together will form a lethal bond of understanding with your target audience, and backed up by eternal wisdom from on high, it will build a communicative platform from which God can call forth His elect.

"Be a yardstick of quality. Some people aren't used to an environment where excellence is expected."

– Steve Jobs

"Excellence is an art won by training and habituation. We do not act rightly because we have virtue or excellence, but we rather have those because we have acted rightly. We are what we repeatedly do. Excellence, then, is not an act but a habit."

– Aristotle

Chapter 19. Rule #9: 10x.

"As for every matter of wisdom and understanding about which the king consulted them, he found them [Daniel and his amigos] ten times better than all the magicians and conjurers who were in all his realm."

— Daniel 1:20

Wow. Imagine that. Christians who're ten times better than the unscrubbed general populace. Yep, that's what the Holy Spirit preserved in the book of Daniel for all of us poor dullards to read, weep and aspire towards.

Now that's a tall order, ladies and gents.

Ten times better than your heathen competition?

No doubt some are thinking, "Garsh … that's not nice, Jesus. Why would you make the standard to influence an anti-theistic environment so hard? I thought Christianity was all about getting stuff, having you bless all our stupid wishes and then going to heaven to eat ice cream with Moses as we play harps, wear white peignoirs and lounge on clouds?"

By the way, that accolade of being "ten times better" was given by a very wicked king and not Danny's mommy nor his doting youth pastor.

Oh, and here's another aside, in case you've never been around powerful and wicked people: they don't give a rat's backside about what you believe. They care about how you perform, how you can benefit them and not if you see angels, wear Christian T-shirts and can speak in tongues. Daniel and his buddies' skill set simply blew Neb away. They were ten times better than all the rest. Just let that sink in a bit …

Here's a question for you, the Christian: I wonder if your "evil" boss, or your "godless" workmates, or your "unsaved" in-laws or family, or your "lost" neighbors, or pretty much every "unwashed" heathen who interfaces with you on a regular basis can say of your work, your craft, your family, your marriage, your appearance, your demeanor and wisdom that you are "tens times better" than all the "estranged from the covenant" peeps who're currently schlepping this third rock from the sun?

Ouch, eh?

Nebuchadnezzar said that about Danny and the boys, and that, my dear reader, is what we're aspiring to in this slim tome, namely: outperforming the lost competition in the practical and honorable stuff of life and work.

Christianity hasn't put too much stock in proclaiming excellence in all our endeavors. No, indeed, we put forth haggard crap and sloppy lives and then we stand back and are aghast that no one wants to listen to us talk about Jesus.

Why should they listen to such a person? Jesus, evidently, hasn't made that big of a difference in their life so ... why should they follow their lead? It's kind of like what Jonathan Edwards' sang about back in 1971, *"But he can't even run his own life, I'll be damned if he'll run mine ..."*

Pedro put it this way ...

> *"Therefore, putting aside all malice and all deceit and hypocrisy and envy and all slander, like newborn babies, long for the pure milk of the word, so that by it you may grow in respect to salvation ... But you are a cho-*

sen race, a royal priesthood, a holy nation, a people for God's own possession, so that you may proclaim the excellencies of Him who has called you out of darkness into His marvelous light ..."

1st Peter 2:1-2,9

Peter, via the inspiration of the Holy Spirit, said the whole point of our getting converted was not going to heaven but an earthly, yea, bodily, proclamation of the excellencies of God.

Jesus spun it in this manner:

"Let your light shine before men in such a way that they may see your good works, and glorify your Father who is in heaven."

Matthew 5:16

Good works (operative word "good"), equates God the Father getting glorified. Shoddy works? Eh ... not so much.

So, what is excellence? Well, excellence simply defined is:

The quality of being outstanding or extremely good. Synonyms include: distinction, quality, superiority, brilliance, greatness, merit, caliber, eminence, preeminence, supremacy; skill, talent, virtuosity, accomplishment, mastery.

Does that define your person and work?

For those who're thinking that excellence is some form of elitism that only the hoity toity care about and it's not an essential and expected quality for all Christians, allow me to slay that notion by stating that excellence isn't about arrogance and ego, but about love for God and an act of worship.

Here's what I mean …

"Whatever you do, do your work heartily, as for the Lord rather than for men, knowing that from the Lord you will receive the reward of the inheritance. It is the Lord Christ whom you serve."

Colossians 3: 23-24

Pablo said our work, whatever it may be, is to be done "heartily" (literally: with our soul) unto God and not just for men. That smacks of excellence to *moi*. Does it to you? *Oui?* Good.

Ergo, hearty and excellent, well done and well made work, is not something that's vanity or an aside to the "more spiritual" matters of evangelism, saying prayers and singing Hillsong's songs.

Hard and smart work is worship; it is to God and for God. Can you imagine actually presenting what you work on, whether it's goods, services or merchandise unto Jesus Christ? Do you think he'd be impressed? Do think he'd be insulted? Do you think he'd say, "Oy vey" and slowly leave your demonstration to go get a glass of wine to try to cheer himself up after watching your presentation?

I'm afraid many Christians would be too embarrassed to show their work to Jesus because it's half-hearted garbage. If your work is crap I guarantee your supposed "personal relationship" with Jesus is crap also. One cannot divorce the two.

For Daniel and his pals, being "just okay", or "good enough", or "nice", was not good enough for them. God deserve their best and the wicked King honored only excellence and, boy howdy … did those boys supply excellence in spades.

The bottom line, with a lot of folks outside Jesus' fold is, "Excellence talks and bullocks walks."

Nebuchadnezzar paid attention to Daniel's counsel because he trumped the competition.

I think the world would give a big ear to what we have to say if our wisdom, work and ways just simply amazed people.

"Do you see a man skilled in his work? He will stand before kings; He will not stand before obscure men."

Proverbs 22:29

Un homme avec Dieu est toujours dans la majorite - "One man with God is always a majority."

– John Knox

Chapter 20. Rule #10:
Pray Like the 3rd Monkey Trying to Get on Noah's Ark

"So I gave my attention to the Lord God to seek Him by prayer and supplications, with fasting, sackcloth and ashes. I prayed to the Lord my God and confessed…"

Daniel 9:3,4

Believer – are you awake to the fact that having significant influence in an atheistic environment is going to take more than your not watching porn videos, drinking Jose Cuervo and smoking crack?

Huh?

These are givens.

These are musts.

The believer, in his negation of obviously negative behavioral traits, must also -- like Daniel – take care of his body and his mind in a theological context, thereby developing an understanding of the world-view and cultural biases of the society that God has called him to reach.

Nevertheless, the believer, though physically fit, mentally astute and culturally *au courant*, must realize that this is still not a "might or power" war he's waging with the powers of darkness. He must be mightily empowered by the Spirit of the living God to affect the changes the situation demands.

This is where prayer and personal holiness figure into righting the wrongs of our current Babylon. An intimate relationship with our Holy God paves the way to a public display of His power over unholy spirits.

You know, we are just plain silly if we think that just because we're hip, smart and now we're well-groomed that demons are all of a sudden afraid of us. Those changes are necessary, but they alone will not dislodge demons from environments that have long been their homes.

Come on, Christian – *we* don't give up *our* stuff that easily, do we?

So, get it straight: demons aren't going to be evicted from their domains just because we are now a little more savvy than the previous batch of religious indolents. Even with the greatest preparation of brains, body and interpersonal skills – it's not enough to win this war. This war is one waged in an unseen realm in which true devotion to the Lordship of Christ and fervent, Christ-centered prayer is the only hope for defeating the enemy.

All this talk of influencing Babylon would be incomplete without my making noise about Daniel's personal piety and his devotion to God in prayer. Think about it, Believer: when the enemy was looking for stuff with which to incriminate Daniel, there was only one thing for which they could bust him: he was violating the king's edict by maintaining his prayer time.

Daniel was committed to excellence in all things, including fervent, intercessory prayer. Daniel had to pray.

You and I have to pray because we stand less than a snowball's chance in Miami against the forces of hell if we aren't gathering the Spirit's strength from the secret place of prayer.

We cannot allow the effects of a secular society to make prayer seem as if it is a non-essential ingredient to the reforming of our culture. Changing society in this post-modern techno age is a complicated venture – one that should heighten our sense of commitment to prayer, rather than relegate it to the back burner of our to-do-list.

With the exponential changes that are on top of the Church like Michael Moore on a case of jelly doughnuts, we must retire often with God in prayer in order to re-emerge in the public square with the goods necessary to straighten out a twisted society.

My wife and I had the privilege of spending a good deal of time with the late Leonard Ravenhill, a man whose prayer life and walk with God makes my devotion to Christ seem lame at best. This great prophet of God was an incredible evangelist, a powerful conference speaker and a prolific author. But the thing that struck me was his prayer life.

Above all things, this was a man who walked with God, and that's the way he would have wanted to be remembered. I heard him pray publicly, and I was privileged to pray with him alone in his study – he was the real deal. I want to let his authority speak regarding the importance of prayer by closing with a passage from one of his best-selling books, *Why Revival Tarries* (a must read, by the way).

Why Revival Tarries, first published in 1962, is a powerful exhortation to young adults to wage our current spiritual war in the strength of our Lord and with the power of His might:

No man is greater than his prayer life. The pastor who is not praying is playing; the people who are not praying are straying. The pulpit can be a shop window to display one's talents; the prayer closet allows no showing off.

Poverty-stricken as the Church is today in many things, she is most stricken here, in the place of prayer. We have many organizers, but few agonizers; many players and payers, few pray-ers; many singers, few clingers; lots of pastors, few wrestlers; many fears, few tears; much fashion, little passion; many interferers, few intercessors; many writers, but few fighters. Failing here, we fail everywhere.

The two prerequisites to successful Christian living are vision and passion, both of which are born and maintained by prayer. The ministry of preaching is opened to few; the ministry of prayer – the highest ministry of all human offices – is open to all. Spiritual adolescents say, "I'll not go tonight, it's only a prayer meeting." It may be that Satan has little cause to fear most preaching. Yet past experiences sting him to rally all his infernal army to fight against God's people praying. Modern Christians know little of binding and loosing, though the onus is on us ... "Whatsoever ye shall bind..." Have you done any of this lately? God is not prodigal with His power; to be much for God, we must be much with God.

Prayer is profoundly simple and simply profound.

Prayer is the simplest form of speech that infant lips can try, yet so sublime that it outranges all speech and can exhaust man's vocabulary.

Can any deny that in the modern church setup the main cause of anxiety is money? Yet that which tries modern churches the most, troubles the New Testament Church the least. Our accent is on paying, and theirs was on praying. When we have paid, the place is taken; when they had prayed, the place was shaken!

In the matter of New Testament, Spirit-inspired, hell-shaking, world-breaking prayer, never has so much been left by so many few. For this kind of prayer there is no substitute.

We do it – or die!

PART FOUR:

Onward Through the Fog

"Why are the nations in an uproar And the peoples devising a vain thing? The kings of the earth take their stand and the rulers take counsel together against the Lord and against His Anointed, saying, "Let us tear their fetters apart and cast away their cords from us!" He who sits in the heavens laughs, The Lord scoffs at them. Then He will speak to them in His anger and terrify them in His fury ..."

– Psalm 2:1-5

Chapter 21. Be Assured, Heaven Rules

"... your kingdom will be assured to you after you recognize that it is Heaven that rules. Therefore, O king, may my advice be pleasing to you: break away now from your sins by doing righteousness and from your iniquities by showing mercy to the poor, in case there may be a prolonging of your prosperity..."

– Daniel 4:26,27

For the majority of Christians, the book of Daniel seems like a truly freaky ecstasy trip. For them, it's one bizarre vision after another. Wild images, vague statements and puzzling dates seem to be the things that occupy the believer's mind when he delves into this book – and for good reason. It's filled with them.

Yet, there is another message that runs through the book of Daniel, and you don't need a *Windtalker* to unravel it. This message is: "Be assured – Heaven rules." The book of Daniel is incredibly plain in the sense that its message unequivocally states that God is in charge of history and that His kingdom will prevail – no matter how bad it gets. Daniel shows the importance of history more clearly than any other portion of the Bible, and it tells us how to live in times of demonic oppression … times like our own.

To think that Daniel is only a 10,000-piece jigsaw puzzle designed by Quentin Tarantino munching blotter and that we are doomed to put it together blind-folded, is to miss its extraordinary relevance for us. While preparing for writing this manuscript, I came across a book by James Boice that explores the book of Daniel. In the preface of his book, Boice mentions five distinct features of Daniel with significance for us today. Consider these facts:

1. Daniel was a godly man sent to live in ungodly Babylon at a time when God's blessing upon the Jewish nation seemed to have been withdrawn or postponed. In short, his position was much like the believer's trying to live in a secular society today.

2. The Babylon of Daniel's day was like all the kingdoms and other countries that either do not acknowledge God or think that they can dispense with Him. This is an apt description of most of the world in our time, including so-called "Christian" America.

3. Daniel and his three Hebrew friends were under tremendous pressure to conform. That is, their religion was tolerated, even respected, as long as they did not allow it to intrude into public life or "rock the boat" of the state. That is our situation also. We can practice our religion so long as it is not in the schools, in the workplace or in any other public place. We have to keep it on the reservation.

4. The world seemed to be winning. King Nebuchadnezzar (and Belshazzar after him) reigned. Nebuchadnezzar believed himself to be above all, having to answer to nobody.

5. Nevertheless, in spite of these things, God told Daniel it is He, God, in control of history, and His purposes are being accomplished – even in the overthrow and captivity of His people. Moreover, in the end God will establish a kingdom to endure forever. The destiny of the people of God is wrapped up in that eternal kingdom.

Daniel and his friends thrived in such circumstances because of their revelation of God's rule over the affairs of men, the fact that He will humble those who walk in pride and the fact that He will shatter every kingdom that exalts itself above the knowledge of God – in His own time.

It's imperative that Christians, especially our youth who are growing up in similar spiritual circumstances as Daniel, have a biblical view of history. Most folks in the Church have such a low view of the sovereignty of God that any manifestation of evil, any change in the jet stream, any earthquake or an elevation of a crooked politician to a place of power, and they're ready to give up and give in. They view such manifestations as the end of the world and the progression of satanic hosts instead of a blip in history that will ultimately work out for the good (for those who love God, at least).

God's rule, His protection of His people and the destruction leveled at those who suppress righteousness and exalt wickedness is all over the pages of the Bible. Every enemy that opposed Him, every negative sanction He imposed to chastise His people, every bad situation and all horrific judgments – everything – served His purpose of purifying His body, exalting His might and exonerating His word.

In time, He rules and His eternal purpose will be brought into a greater manifestation. Show me one time in the Bible when God didn't have the last laugh. Young man, young woman … you have got to get that revelation digested into your spirit if you are going to overcome the powers of darkness in your time.

"The gods had condemned Sisyphus to ceaselessly rolling a rock to the top of a mountain, whence the stone would fall back of its own weight. They had thought with some reason that there is no more dreadful punishment than futile and hopeless labor."

– Albert Camus

Chapter 22. History:
It's Greek to Me

The views of history held by the majority of Christians are nothing more than pagan mindsets. There are two views of history that you as a Christian must absolutely reject. And no, I don't care if your grandmother believed them.

The first of these is found among the ancient Greeks. The Greeks had what may be called a "cyclical" view of history. They thought all events were nothing more than endless, repeated cycles. In other words, what is happening today will someday be repeated. The good will become bad, and the bad will become good; what goes around comes around. There is no meaning, and there is no progress. This premise promotes the impossibility of finding any real meaning or progress in history. This point of view states that history has no goal. You may have a goal, but history does not.

Another name for this philosophy is nihilism, i.e., history is essentially meaningless, nothingness. Moreover, laboring to alter it is an exercise in futility. John Marsh has given a great synopsis of the Greek view of history in his book, *In the Fullness of Time*:

From the nature of their cosmology it was perhaps impossible for the Greeks to develop anything other than a cyclical view of history. The great age of the world would one day begin all over again, and the cycle of events would be repeated.

If such a view be true, then historical existence has been deprived of its significance. What I do now I have done in a previous world cycle and will do again in the future world cycles. Responsibility and decisions disappear, and with them any real significance to historical life, which in fact becomes a rather grandiose natural cycle. Just as the corn is sown, grows and ripens each year, so will the events of history recur time after time.

Moreover, if all that can happen is the constant repetition of an event-cycle, there is no possibility of meaning in the cycle itself. It achieves nothing in itself, neither can it contribute to anything outside itself.

In short, the events of history are devoid of significance. Therefore, the Greeks couldn't conceive of history itself as being purposeful or as leading to a goal. For the Greeks, time and history represented a realm from which one longed to be delivered. Because the Greeks thought that life was enslavement and that existence, in time, was a curse. Redemption to the Greek would be outside of time and history, rather than within it.

The Greeks' view of history is incompatible with the Christian view, which sees history as an unfolding of God's eternal purpose that is moving toward His goal (mentioned in Ephesians 1:1-10) of "the summing up of all things in Christ, things in heaven and things upon the earth."

The canonical writers didn't see history as meaningless. They saw history as moving toward God's irresistible, persistent, eternal purpose that nothing can thwart. History, according to the writers of the Bible, had a goal, and every act of God – both positive and negative – that occurred on this planet serves Jehovah's divine desires. This didn't cause a cyclical recurrence of mere nothingness, but an upward, linear, progressive development of His glory and goals that are in accord with His eternal counsel.

If you think you are beaten, you are
If you think you dare not, you don't,
If you like to win, but you think you can't
It is almost certain you won't.

If you think you'll lose, you're lost
For out of the world we find,
Success begins with a fellow's will
It's all in the state of mind.

– Walter D. Wintle

Chapter 23. We Preached Defeat and We Got It

"Hope deferred makes the heart sick…"

– Proverbs 13:12

The second interpretation of history that we need to flush down the toilet is that of atheistic existentialism. This type of existentialism also states that history is without meaning. Their apologists blather on about history having no significant pattern, no movement towards a goal – only a meaningless succession of events.

If this is true, the only thing left is raw individualism: every man for himself.

Man, according to this point of view, must try to find his way from a non-authentic life to an authentic existence by making significant decisions. Simply put, atheistic existentialism believes that while personal heroic actions may bring meaning to the individual's life and help him for a while, it will have no permanent significance in history. Significant acts authenticate the individual's life but have no causal alteration of history.

This pessimistic existential view of history is also opposed to the biblical paradigm. Without denying the importance of the individual getting his or her life authenticated, Scripture does see meaning in history. God is working out His plan in history. It doesn't matter whether things look grim or incredibly hopeful. God's purpose grinds on, ever developing, ever unfolding.

Although the Christian may freely admit that redemption has come about in time, many view time as a meaningless slavery from which they long to be freed. They long to be raptured out of this mess. They wish Christ would hurry up and come back.

Most Christians aren't looking to the second coming of Jesus because of their love for Him, but rather out of sheer hopelessness and the avoidance of responsibility to actively engage their culture in difficult times the way Daniel did. Indeed, because most Christians have been programmed by false teaching to expect the triumph of Satan in time and history, they think that whatever they try to do will ultimately be undone, with their efforts making little difference in the great scheme of things. They erroneously assume that in time, Satan wins.

Redemption, to Christians with this mindset, has little ramification historically. They think we must wait until we get to heaven to see any true restoration, either personally or globally. Hendrikus Berkof said:

> *The average Christian does not expect to see any positive signs of Christ's reign in the world. He believes that the world only becomes worse and worse and races in the direction of the antichrist ... The average Christian is not aware of the presence of the kingdom in the world today...*

> *Prevalent in our churches is the bad kind of pietism ... which limits the power of Christ to His personal relationship to the individual believer, and which sees no connection between Christ and world events, or between Christ and daily work. This leads to an ungrateful blindness for the signs of Christ's reign in the present. Expressions such as "we live on the edge of a volcano," "it can't last this way much longer," "humanity is steadily becoming worse" and "the end of time is near" are very popular in many Christian circles. And they believe that this pessimism toward their culture ... is completely is agreement with their Christian faith.*

So, now that I've slammed a couple of erroneous views of history and also tweaked the Christian's cheek for believing nonsense, let's define what a Christian view of history should be. This is what will help you as a young adult to have hope in times of darkness, what will spur you on to discipline and faith as you are acutely aware that the adversity you are now facing is ultimately serving His purpose. Therefore, don't despair and don't whine; because, according to the Scripture, God rules in time.

Christianity and history have always been allies. Leopold Von Ranke's observation that history convinces more people than philosophy is certainly confirmed by the Christian response to this discipline. The Bible contains a great deal more history than philosophy. Christianity is rooted in history, and without its historical roots, there would be no Christian worldview.

Nearly all of human history, from the Christian perspective, can be summarized by reference to relatively few landmark historical events. Consider the following:

- The revelation of God, primarily His intelligence and power, through the creation of heaven and earth (Gen. 1.1).

- The special creation of male and female as body, soul and spirit (Gen. 1.26-28).

- The rebellion of mankind against His creator (Gen. 3.1-5).

- The revelation of God through the patriarchs (Abraham, Isaac and Jacob) and Israel (primarily, the Old Testament).

- The crossing of the Red Sea.

- The appearance of God in history in the person of Jesus Christ to redeem mankind from sin (1 Tim. 3.16).

- The resurrection of Jesus Christ (1 Cor. 15).

- The revelation of God through His Church, the Body of Christ (primarily, the New Testament).

- The judgment of the world (Acts 17.31).

- The new heavens, the new earth and the new Jerusalem for the redeemed of all ages (Rev. 21).

Christian history has past, present and future characteristics. Christians adhere to a linear, rather than a cyclical, view. David Noebel says that:

For Christians, the Bible is a work of beauty and truth – a word from God concerning His love for creation – not a work of myth or legend. The Bible accurately describes events that actually occurred in history. Twentieth century archaeology generally reinforces biblical history, including the Mosaic authorship of the Pentateuch, the historicity of the patriarchs and the Exodus, as well as the historical background concerning the virgin birth, sinless life, vicarious death and physical resurrection of Jesus Christ.

Of course, St. Paul's statement regarding history in 1 Corinthians 10, "I would not have you to be ignorant of (history)," is a solid base for a philosophy of history. Christians are certainly exhorted to learn from history (1 Cor. 10.11). St. Paul also made it very clear that if Christ were not raised from the dead, there would be no Christian faith. Christians view the resurrection of Christ as an historical event occurring in Jerusalem sometime between AD 30 and AD 33.

Stephen's defense of the faith in Acts 7 is a lesson in history. Luke, the author of two books of the Bible (Luke and Acts), was a meticulous historian. The historical Bible (the written word of God) and Jesus Christ (the Living Word) are the two cornerstones of the Christian worldview. If the Bible is not history, or if Jesus Christ is not "God with us," then Christianity crumbles; therefore, Christians need to invest a great deal of time and effort strengthening and defending both of these foundational stones.

It is the Christian position that it takes less faith to believe that God created the heavens and the earth and all things therein, than to believe that everything is a result of chance.

Christians understand God to have created history when He created time, and they believe that God also has the ability to control the universe and bring history to a fitting close.

As young adults poised to make an impact on the earth during this tumultuous new millennium, we must understand what all the great reformers believed and understood:

1. History is a working out of God's purposes.

2. God is Lord of history, even turning evil into His ultimate good.

3. Christ is the center of history. We date our calendars, numbering the years forward and backward from His birth. Thus, the whole of history and how the majority of the world perceives it is completely, if subliminally, dominated by Jesus Christ.

4. The new age has already been ushered in; God's kingdom has come and is coming.

And lastly, all of history is moving toward a goal: the new heavens and the new earth.

PART FIVE:

Here's Some Other Stuff to Consider

"One must avoid snobbery and misanthropy. But one must also be unafraid to criticise those who reach for the lowest common denominator, and who sometimes succeed in finding it. This criticism would be effortless if there were no "people" waiting for just such an appeal. Any fool can lampoon a king or a bishop or a billionaire. A trifle more grit is required to face down a mob, or even a studio audience that has decided it knows what it wants and is entitled to get it."

– Christopher Hitchens

Chapter 24. Dear Parents, Pastors and Mentors: Teach Your Young People to Righteously Rebel

---

"The Passover of the Jews was near, and Jesus went up to Jerusalem. And He found in the temple those who were selling oxen and sheep and doves, and the money changers seated at their tables. And He made a scourge of cords, and drove them all out of the temple, with the sheep and the oxen; and He poured out the coins of the money changers and overturned their tables; and to those who were selling the doves He said, 'Take these things away; stop making My Father's house a place of business.' His disciples remembered that it was written, 'Zeal for Your house will consume me.' "

– John 2:13-17

Dear Parents, Pastors and Mentors: Sometimes, when the twaddle gets egregious, we've got to teach our young charges to revolt against its purveyors.

As you know, for the last several decades there has been a belligerent, systematic secularization of the United States by the liberal thought police. These individuals have sought to remove from all public sectors of society any semblance of biblical values, all influence of religious institutions, all sacred symbolism and the traditional core values which have made America great. A Cyclops can see that.

Of the many mental illnesses the secularists suffer from, two primary pains motivate them to work against the universe: 1) a repulsion from God and 2) a massive American History memory loss.

Being saddled with these illnesses, instead of seeking healing or having an exorcism or joining MA (Misguided Anonymous) or just moving to Holland where they'll be nice and comfy, they have chosen rather to create a new United States of Sassy Secularists in which the traditionalist is kicked to the curb and their novel material girls get to govern.

To accomplish the creation of the USSS, they have become busy monkeys trying to level authorities, rewrite records, become judge and jury of all things everywhere, homogenize cultures, pimp style over substance and deify power while they prop up the "victims of the system" to drive their imagined American magic bus.

On Planet Secularity where "truth is dead," muscle-power becomes the operative standard of speech. The results are cultic conformity and group bullying. The chief goal of the secular sellers of societal swill is to create a rock-solid environment of political correctness -- with the intended end being the cowing of people who might rustle their feathers by not parroting their already tried (and been found wanting) opinions. They can't allow people to speak and think freely because the realist and the truth dealer would ruin their little party.

Therefore, the person who champions a traditional view of truth (not propaganda), who stands for the historical record (not the hysterical read) and who believes that biblically-based, previously proven and transcendent standards should continue to serve as an external pattern to govern our nation's character will endure more scorn than Ted Nugent crashing Rosie's pool party. (That was a very rough Dougified paraphrase from an Os Guinness speech. No offense, Os.).

However, the secularist's opposition to the Christian's values shouldn't rattle the righteous rebel. No, this brazen attack by bloviators should actually turn on the upright dissenter. The faithful Christian who loves God and the way this nation was originally

constituted will joyfully stand up against this hijack-
ing of our nation by the "progressive" Philistines.
Yes, the grand and the noble young person will not
lie down and roll up like an opossum just because
the truth isn't *en vogue*. Great people side with truth
even when it's detested.

The believer, who is worth their salt, will not roll
up in the fetal position and wet their big Christian di-
aper because they're being opposed. No sir. No way.
Not now. Not ever. Rather, the hardy follower of The
Rebel from Galilee, will continue to speak out, work
hard and self sacrifice in order to preserve classic traditional Judeo-Christian values.

As stated, we need, as in right now, young people,
who hold to traditional values to become rebels with
a cause. The problem is, however, most people with
family values/faith have become too nice to fight in
the public arena for God's grand principles.

Yes, somehow a large chunk of the church has
embraced a feckless faith, lead by a cardigan wearing Nancy-boy Jesus and have contented themselves
with being tolerant doormats for dillweeds with
dense ideas. I, on the other hand, don't play that
game because, as I see it, I serve a great God whose
principles are not to be compromised and are worth
defending and passing on.

The reality is, young person, you have been birthed in the midst of a raging culture war where time-honored principles are being thrashed. The chances of our kids inheriting an America like we have been blessed with are slim.

No doubt some of you are having a hard time trying to square being a Christian and being a righteous rabble rouser against the secular naysayers.

It could be because you have drunk the courage killing poisonous doctrine brewed by libs -- namely that Jesus is one big wuss. As I have stated many times throughout my writing career, I believe a significant portion of the church has bought into the notion that if you're a Christian you're supposed to be accepting of whatever crud culture crams down our throat. And that's what a nice Christian should do. Could you be a gobbler of this toxic waste?

The secularists love to propagate their malleable image of Christ to Christians, i.e. the sweet, bearded lady, definitely cowed Jesus who is always accommodating and never dissenting, a veritable stained glass Gumby who'll bend when pressured.

Yep, the secularists joyfully tout this unbiblical, emasculated image of Immanuel to their ilk, and a lot of the church is stupid enough to gulp it down and ask for seconds. The anti-theistic thought police love it when Christians buy into this perversion of Jesus' person and work as it makes them squishy dolts that are easily controlled.

If, as parents, pastors and mentors with biblical values, we want our kids to have a fair to middling chance that the USA, which they will inherit, will bear some semblance of its former glory and greatness, then I believe (first and foremost) we have got to dispense with this candy cane Christ that we have been sold.

One way to do this, dad, is to grab a Bible, a highlighter and your kids and go through the Scripture and mark every counterculture and confrontational thing Christ did when he cruised this planet. The pages will quickly turn fluorescent yellow, and you will swiftly be blown away by the ubiquitous examples of Jesus' "unChrist-like" behavior. After you blow through the gospels with your offspring reading with a special eye toward the rebel texts, then do this:

1. Apologize to your child for ever thinking, and maybe even teaching, the heretical concept that Jesus was a pushover and lastly . . .

2. Let the power of the Scripture and the Holy Spirit purge forever the notion from your soul that Jesus was a Twinkie who put up with

political, cultural and ecclesiastical nonsense.

For example: Here's what I, the proud President of The Testosterone Fog Club, get when I read about Jesus in the gospels and the Book of Revelation, and this is what I brought to my little Bible "studies" with my daughters when they were young:

- When Jesus Christ got injected into the human mix two thousand-plus years ago, from the cradle to the cross, He was a lightning rod of controversy. His incarnation heated up the culture war.

- Immanuel's arrival upon the scene caused demon-inspired political idiots to try to kill Him while He was still cooing and pooping in His pampers. The dragon no likey his party getting ruined, and ruin it the Prince of Peace did.

- The initial message the Wonderful Counselor preached, according to Dr. Luke's take, ticked off the crowd He was addressing so thoroughly that they attempted to throw Him off a cliff. He nailed that haughty mob for the crud they were practicing -- and He did so publicly. Yes, in public. Ouch. That's not very "Christian" of Christ!

- In reality (on this planet), Jesus received

minimal accolades. No lucrative gigs with the Premier Speakers Bureau; no "isn't He so nice! Let's put Him on Oprah" invite; no fat, Creflo Dollar like honorariums; no limousine chariot services. He got nada, nothing, zilch, zero, zippo -- and for those who haven't seen *The Passion of the Christ* yet, it sorta got even uglier.

- The truth of the matter is that what Jesus said and did caused more discomfort to man's me-monkey human spirit than cheap Tequila and three bags of pork rinds drenched in hot sauce would to Martha Stewart's tummy. I made it clear to my girls that today, in our radically wussified, politically correct state of bland, our culture wouldn't embrace the Christ of Scripture because He'd get under our skin. And we love our skin.

I believe one of the reasons Christians have spawned capitulating softies is because the masculine leaders have ducked out of the spiritual equation of their kids. Yes, the chances are extremely high that if a man's input is absent or lacking, that his kids' spirituality will take on an imbalanced, effeminate quality and will be minus the rowdy, rebel funk that men bring to the table; and they will therefore be non-resistant "believers" in the face of every addle-pate's bad ideas.

I'm convinced that the Christian man, who's not ashamed of his masculinity, will by fiat make young people under his tutelage staunch combatants for Christian values -- just as his Savior was. Yep, I'm sold on the precept that if one truly follows Jesus, that they not only will be graceful to the sinful but will also be antagonistic to the obstreperous who won't break with their idiocy. Especially when the bad ideas detrimentally affect multitudes.

So, parents, pastors and mentors: teach young people to be nice, to mind their own business, to help old ladies across the street, but realize that you and the youth are alive in the midst of a raging culture war. You must realize that Jesus wasn't "nice" all the time and neither should you be, especially when His standards today are getting the same treatment that a fire hydrant gets from a dog.

Where and How to Raze a Little Hell

The chief point of assault upon your kids is going to be via government schools, as the secularists have officially hijacked these institutes and have turned them into the main source of their misinformation indoctrination. This will be the first major battlefield in their life. If they survives this fray with their Judeo-Christian values intact, they'll be one heck of a warrior for the rest of their life.

Hear me well, dad: If you're going to send your child to a public school or a state run university, then you've got to teach your young one not to just sit there in class being a good kid and taking whatever propaganda the secular "progressives" shove down their throat. You must teach them to deftly defy defunct dogmas and not turn a blind eye to bad ideas.

Yes, you've got to teach your child to feel proud and comfortable with not being a communist, with believing in God, with our nation's spiritual heritage and with not having their genitals turned into a campus Jiffy Lube. At today's universities, your college student will be a radical if they don't lock step to the liberal dogma.

For those students who wish to make a dent on their campus, not only for their sake but for the following generations, I have 10 things you must do if you want to be an effective agent of change on your campus:

1. Get a sense of humor. Most liberal profs and student activists are a screeching, nerve-grating, nasally bunch of whiners. As a matter of fact, I'd rather watch Maxine Waters do jumping jacks in Borat's thong than listen to the hemp-clothed, goatee bearing, chunky liberal bleat. Therefore, conservative student, when you queue up to address your crowd, be pleasant,

poke fun at yourself, remove the whine from your voice and use honed humor to humiliate the Left. Getting folks to laugh at your opponents and not being rabid about taking yourself so seriously helps get your point across.

2. Get creative. God bless technology. Young rebels, you have at your fingertips the wherewithal to go creatively crazy for the cause of God and country with the real possibility of a stack of people seeing and hearing what you have to offer. Therefore, get nutty with your stuff. Utilize these amazing techno tools to tackle the tools on the Left. Take your gift, your talent, your voice and your God-wired weirdness and put something artistic out there that'll overtly or covertly slamdance the radical leftists who seek to sabotage our society.

3. Get tough. One thing that drives me nuts about some "Christians" is their bemoaning how they get attacked when they go public in the classroom with their sentiments.

   Boo-hoo, you little baby. What did you think the anti-theistic professors were going to do, clap? Buy you candy? Look, not-so-sharp holder of biblical values, we're in a very real culture war. The crud will hit the fan when you counter their lunacy in the classroom. Embrace it. Suck it up. Get tough. Let adversity be your Wheaties, the breakfast of champions.

4. Get prayerful. Most folks on the ludicrous left who embrace what 21st century liberals currently spew are admitted atheists. Seeing that they don't believe in the God who is, I'm a guessin' they are probably not down the funnel with the discipline of prayer. That is, until they're about to die. Then, of course, they start praying like Kevin Hart freshly filled with the Holy Ghost and fire. Since they refuse to believe and pray to God, they have no supernatural help in their hapless cause. At least no positive supernatural help because we all know demons love to assist these guys. But I digress...

So ... God-fearing rebel, ask God for a) crazy clout to change yourself so that you're not a wastoid He's got to work around and b) for a dynamic enabling to effect constructive change on your campus and culture. To upgrade your prayer life, get E. M. Bounds' classic, *Power Through Prayer*.

5. Get informed. Christian contrarians, you've got to get the following books and read them:

The Politically Incorrect Guide to American History,

The Politically Incorrect Guide to Darwinism and Intelligent Design,

The Politically Incorrect Guide to English and American Literature,

The Politically Incorrect Guide to Global

Warming and Environmentalism,

The Politically Incorrect Guide to Islam (and the Crusades),

The Politically Incorrect Guide to Science,

The Politically Incorrect Guide to the Constitution,

The Politically Incorrect Guide to the South (and Why It Will Rise Again),

The Politically Incorrect Guide to Women, Sex, and Feminism, and ...

Digest the above and when appropriate, take some of the factoids found within these liberalism-devastating tomes and share them with your prof during class and your buddies in the dorm. It's fun for the whole family.

6. Get speakers to your campus who'll fire up your base. You can book me to speak to your group. I'd love to come and toss the cat among the pigeons.

7. Get sharp looking. Most campus Liberals have a monopoly on ugly. They are neither pleasing to the ear nor eye. Do not follow their lead, young rebel. If they want to look slovenly, unshorn and tie-dyed, let 'em. You, however, should run in the opposite direction.

Don't believe that smack about looks don't

matter. The heck they don't. If I have the choice between these two options: 1) to look at and listen to an obese girl with frizzed out hair and so many piercings that it looks like a tackle box blew up in her face, or 2) to look at and listen to a svelte, well-put-together, conscientious girl graciously appealing to me, I am telling you right here and now that I'll choose #2. The nasty girl has offended my senses, lost my attention, and I couldn't care less what she has to say. Call me crazy.

8. Get your grades up.

9. Get your hands dirty. Serve your campus and community. The world has enough of derisive, hate-filled protests and marches by ideological miscreants. While you're in college, help in the critical areas of your campus and community's needs and watch the campus and community give you a standing O.

"No man is worth his salt who is not ready at all times to risk his well-being, to risk his body, to risk his life, in a great cause."

– Theodore Roosevelt

Appendix 1: The Cultural Acid Test for Pastors

"You are the salt of the earth; but if the salt has become tasteless, how can it be made salty again? It is no longer good for anything, except to be thrown out and trampled under foot by men…"

– Matthew 5:13

The way I see it, the "God job" has two fronts: 1) to reach out to a lost soul helping to keep it from hell and 2) to righteously leaven our current cruddy culture for Christ.

First, Pastors are to study and teach the word of God carefully and apply it to our lives practically, so we don't end up drinking goofy grape and committing suicide *en masse* with the latest Jim Jones cult. Additionally, they are called to help their congregants build the good society in our nation. Y'know, the "Thy will be done on earth as it is in heaven" stuff?

This means you must not focus your attention only on evangelism but also weigh in on all things which affect our culture, e.g, business, entertainment, education and, yes, politics. All the aforementioned directly affect the health and wealth of the people you are trying to reach; and they require that you have a biblically based opinion on each category in order to influence them in ways that honor God.

The culture-dividing issues are obvious; it is mind-boggling that many clergy are mute or side with parties, policies and principles that are antithetical to what Scripture clearly states is holy, just and good. As far as I'm concerned, a silent or waffling pastor in today's climate is a bad guy. I don't care how much he likes kitty cats and candy canes. Look, mute boy, if you're not in the middle of this crucial cultural squabble, then you're Dr. Evil in my book.

In some kind of ascending order, it seems to me there are 10 reasons why pastors avoid political issues and why they are chicken hearted.

1. Fear of man. If you purport to be a man of "the cloth", then your regard for God and His opinion must trump the trepidation of the creature God created from spit and mud. Come on, man of God, don't fear us. We're ants with smart-

phones that'll shoot Botox into our foreheads. We're friggin' weird and fickle weather vanes of the modern media. Lead us ... don't follow us! Never live for a nod from the congregation or some political twerp or a particular party, especially when said group is way off biblical base.

2. Ignorance. Most people are not bold in areas where they are ignorant ... always excepting Nancy Pelosi, of course. I know, keeping up with all the pressing political issues is maddening, but that's life, Dinky; and if you want to be a voice in society and not just an echo, you have got to be in the know. Staying briefed, running each political issue through the gauntlet of Scripture and determining God's mind on a certain subject are par for the course for the hardy world-changer. It's the information age. Get informed and watch your boldness increase.

3. Division. Y'know, I hate the current non-essential divisions in the church as much as the next acerbic Christian author. Squabbling over the color of the carpet, who'll play the organ next Sunday or who is the Beast of Revelation, is stupidity squared. Hey, divisive Christian rebel without a clue -- get a life, *por favor*. Or become a Satanist and go screw up their church. Do something other than make mountains out of your little molehill issues.

That being said, however, there's a time and place for a biblical throw-down and an ecclesiastical split from political policies and parties:

- When the taking of an unborn life is the issue.

- When marriage is being redefined.

- When runaway judges are attempting to expunge God and His law from our country's national life.

For a minister to seek unity with such when they are trashing and rewriting Scripture with impunity is to side with evil and to allow darkness to succeed. On these kinds of issues, the minister cannot group hug such anti-biblical dolts.

4. Last Days Madness. Many ministers do not get involved in political issues because they believe that "it simply doesn't matter" since "the end has come", and Jehovah is about to run the credits on this failed earth flick. These defeatists believe that any change in the jet stream, war, earthquakes, a warming globe, the success of a corrupt politician -- even a new Kim Kardashian special -- are "proof" that God is getting really, really ticked off, and that His only recourse is to have Christ physically return and kick some major butt.

They see the church and themselves as impotent and having no real ability to change things culturally with any long range ramifications. Thus, any stab at a better tomorrow is simply an exercise in futility for this crew. Attempting to right culture is, in their eyes, equivalent to polishing brass on a sinking ship; therefore, they are content to simply tramp from Christian concert to Christian concert, eat fatty foods and stare at Christian videos.

5. Sloth. Classically defined, sloth is lethargy stemming from a sense of hopelessness. Viewing our nation and the world as an irreparable disaster, where our exhortations, prayers, votes and labors will not produce any temporal fruit, leaves one with all the fervor of a normal guy who's forced to French kiss his sister.

If you're wondering why your flock is so apathetic, Pastor Grim Carnage, ask yourself if you have stolen their earthly hope that their valiant efforts can actually prevail in time, and not just in eternity. If you constantly pump the doom and gloom message, if you teach them that evil will ultimately triumph on our *terra firma*, if you spew messages that consciously or unconsciously convey "big, anti-Christ" and "little Jesus Christ", then you have effectively zapped what's left of your parishioners' passion.

6. They don't want to lose their Tax Exempt status. Many pastors, priests and parishioners have been cowed into inactivity by the threatened loss of their tax-exempt status if they say anything remotely political. This can make pastors who don't, or won't, get good legal advice about as politically active as Howard Hughes was during the flu season.

The church may, among other things, register their members to vote, pass out voter guides, invite all candidates in a race to speak (even if only one of them shows up) and speak directly about specific issues.

Off the clock, in his personal capacity, the pastor or priest can endorse and support (or oppose) whomever or whatever he wishes -- like any other citizen. There are no limitations to the individual; the ones that do exist under the 501(c)(3) statute are only for the church entity and/or the pastor in his official capacity, not for the pastor or the members who make up the church. And, as of 2017, Trump took away all the government bullying of churches which speak out publicly about political issues. #maga

7. They bathe in paltry pietism. Pastors avoid politics because such concerns are "unspiritual", and their focus is on the "spirit world". Yes, to such imbalanced ministers, political affairs are seen as "temporal and carnal"

and, because pastors and priests trade in the "eternal and spiritual", such "transient" issues get the same attention from them as Yoko Ono's tuning fork does from her.

This bunch is primarily into heavenly emotions and personal Bible study, and they stay safely tucked away from society and its complicated issues. They forget that they are commanded to be seriously engaged with our culture.

8. They have bought into the Islamic extremist comparison. Pastors have muffled their political voices because they fear being lumped in with Islam by the politically correct thought police. The correlation made between Christians' non-violent attempts at gracious and intelligent policy persuasion and Islam's kill-you-in-your-sleep campaigns is nothing more than pure, uncut crapola.

Ministers, please blow off the tongue-wagging blowhards who try to intimidate you into silence by making quantum, ludicrous, scat-laden and analogous leaps in equating the implementation of a gracious, biblical worldview with the Islam-o-fascists' cross-eyed perspective.

9. They can't say "Heck no!" to minutiae. Some ministers can't get involved in studying or speaking out regarding pressing issues sim-

ply because of the ten tons of junk they are forced to field within their congregations. Spending time wet-nursing 40-year-olds without a life and being bogged down in committee meetings over which shade of pink paint should be used for the Women's Aglow's ministerial wing of their church, ministers are lucky if they get to study the Bible nowadays -- much less anything else.

This is the fault of both the ministers with their messiah complexes and the congregants with their me-monkey syndromes, and they must all have an exorcism (or something) if the church is going to tackle cultural issues.

10. They likey the money. The creepy thing about a lot of ministers is their unwillingness to give political or cultural offense when offense is needed, simply because taking a biblical stand on a political issue might cost them their time-share in Sanibel and their BMW. Oh well, what do you expect? Christ had His Judas, and evangelicalism has its cheap hookers.

Never fear, pastor. Even though nailing your colors to the mast during putrid political times might cost you a parishioner or two, don't sweat it. There are also tens of thousands of serious parishioners who are looking for leaders with the guts to lead the church to make its proper stance during these difficult days

If the ministers within the good old US of A would crucify their fear of man, get solidly briefed regarding the chief political issues, not sweat necessary division, not get caught up in last days madness, maintain their hope for tomorrow, understand their liberties under God and our Constitution, not become so heavenly minded that they're no earthly good, focus on the majors and blow off bowing to cash instead of convictions, then maybe … just maybe … we will see their influence cause our nation to take a righteous turn away from the secularist progressives' putrid pit.

Appendix 2: Read This

"Paul, you are out of your mind! Your great learning is driving you mad. But Paul said, 'I am not out of my mind, most excellent Festus, but I utter words of sober truth…' "

– Acts 26:24,25

In addition to the Bible, devour these bad boys ...

Pussification: The Effeminization Of The American Male, by me.

Paradise Restored, by David Chilton

All the books in Regnery's, Politically Incorrect Guide Series.

Defending Your Faith, by R.C. Sproul.

The Consequences of Ideas, by R.C. Sproul.

Last Days Madness, by Gary Demar.

The Christian In Complete Armour, by William Gurnall.

Precious Remedies Against Satan's Devices, by Thomas Brooks.

Invitation to the Classics: A Guide to Books You've Always Wanted to Read, by Os Guinness & Louis Cowan.

The Call, by Os Guinness.

Addicted to Mediocrity: 20th Century Christians And The Arts, by Franky Schaeffer.

Raising Righteous And Rowdy Girls, by me.

In, But Not Of: A Guide To Christian Ambition, by Hugh Hewitt.

Acknowledgments

Special thanks to Winkie Pratney for making alive the book of Daniel and giving it a brilliant 21st century twist. I heard Winkie minister on this topic just one time during the summer of '95, and it dramatically changed my approach to life, ministry and the secular city. Muchas gracias, Señor Pratney.

About The Author.

Doug Giles is the co-founder and co-host of the *Warriors & Wildmen* podcast (425K downloads in 9months) and the man behind ClashDaily.com. In addition to driving ClashDaily.com (228M page views), Giles is the author of the #1 Amazon.com best-selling book, *PUSSIFI-CATION: The Effeminization of the American Male.*

Doug's writings have appeared on several other print and online news sources, including Townhall.com, The *Washington Times*, The *Daily Caller*, Fox Nation, *USA Today*, The *Wall Street Journal*, The *Washington Examiner*, *American Hunter Magazine* and ABC News.

Giles and his wife Margaret have two daughters, Hannah and Regis. Hannah devastated ACORN with her 2009 nation-shaking undercover videos and she currently stars in the explosive, 2018 Tribeca Documentary, *Acorn And The Firestorm.* Regis is the purveyor of GirlsJustWanna-HaveGuns.com and has been featured in *Elle*, *American Hunter* and *Variety* magazines. Regis is also the author of a powerful new book titled, *How Not To Be A #Me-Too Victim, But A #WarriorChick (White Feather Press-March 2018).* Regis and Hannah are both black belts in Gracie/Valente Jiu Jitsu.

DG's interests include guns, big game hunting, big game fishing, fine art (DougGiles.art), cigars, helping wounded warriors, and being a big pain in the butt to people who dislike God and the USA.

Accolades for Giles include …

Giles was recognized as one of "The 50 Best Conservative Columnists Of 2015".

Giles was recognized as one of "The 50 Best Conservative Columnists Of 2014".

Giles was recognized as one of "The 50 Best Conservative Columnists Of 2013".

ClashDaily.com was recognized as one of "The 100 Most Popular Conservative Web-sites For 2013".

Doug was noted as "Hot Conservative New Media Superman" By Politichicks.

Speaking Engagements

Doug Giles speaks to college, business, community, church, advocacy and men's groups throughout the United States and internationally. His expertise includes issues of Christianity and culture, masculinity vs. metrosexuality, big game hunting and fishing, raising righteous kids in a rank culture, the Second Amendment, personal empowerment, politics, and social change. For availability, please contact us at 'clash@clashdaily.com'. Use 'SPEAKING ENGAGEMENT' for the subject line.

Doug's podcast can be seen and heard at

WarriorsAndWildmen.com.

PUSS-I-FI-CA-TION: The act, or process, of a man being shamed, taught, lead, pastored, drugged or otherwise coerced or cajoled into throwing out his brain, handing over his testicles and formally abandoning the rarefied air of the testosterone-leader-fog that God and nature hardwired him to dwell in, and instead become a weak, effem- inate, mangina sporting, shriveled up little quail. From The Doug Giles 2016 Dictionary of Grow the Heck Up, Tinkerpot! In Giles' latest, and most raucous book, he takes Snowflakes from the warm wet womb of 'Pussville' to the rarefied air of 'Mantown.' This is definitely one of the most politically incorrect books to ever hit the market. It will most certainly offend the entitled whiners, but it will also be a breath of fresh air to young males who wish to be men versus hipster dandies.

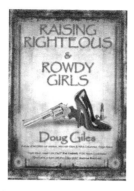

It has been said that daughters are God's revenge on fathers for the kind of men they were when they were young. Some would say that both Doug Giles and I, given our infamous pasts, are charter members of that club. However, Doug and I know that his two wonderful daughters and my equally wonderful daughter and two granddaughters are truly God's fantastic gift. With the wisdom of hindsight and experience Doug has written the ultimate manual for dads on raising righteous and rowdy daughters who will go out into the world well prepared- morally, physically, intellectually and with joyful hearts- to be indomitable and mighty lionesses in our cultural jungle. Through every raucous and no-holds-barred page, Doug, the incomparable Dad Drill Sergeant, puts mere men through the paces to join the ranks of the few, the proud, and the successful fathers of super daughters. The proof of Doug Giles' gold-plated credentials are Hannah and Regis Giles- two of the most fantastic, great hearted and accomplished young ladies I have ever known. This is THE BOOK that I will be giving the father of my two precious five and three year old granddaughters. Tiger Mom meet Lion Dad!

— Pat Caddell

Fox News Contributor —

**Check out Doug's art
work at DougGiles.Art**

Made in the USA
Monee, IL
18 July 2020

36705602R00105